BEHIND EVERY
EVERY
Champion...

KEITH A. ZIMMER

Dageforde Publishing
Lincoln, Nebraska

ISBN: 1-886225-13-3
Library of Congress Number: 96-84295

Cover Art by Angie Johnson Art Productions
Cover reference photo provided by Dennis Hubbard

Original Illustrations by Angie Johnson Art Productions

Photography by Dennis Hubbard; UN-L Photography, Richard Voges, Photographer; B.J. Fictum; Keith Zimmer; and various personal photos of team members. Photo of Keith Zimmer on dust jacket by Eric Giebler.

Printed in the United States of America.

Dageforde Publishing
941 'O' Street, Suite 728
Lincoln, Nebraska 68508-3625
(402) 475-1123

DEDICATION

During the 1995 season, as one of five team captains for the Nebraska football team, I often had the chance to have the last words in the locker room before our team took the field. Now, I am honored to have the last words before you read this book. *Behind Every Champion...* is special to me and my twenty senior teammates. The stories you will read are about the people behind the Nebraska football players. Our lives have been forever changed because of the Nebraska football experience. For some, including me, there have been ups and downs. Yet, we have never given up on our goals and dreams. Through unity we became champions on the field and I know all of us will become champions in life.

First and foremost, the 1995 Nebraska football seniors would like to dedicate this book to our head coach, Dr. Tom Osborne. He has been a father figure to each and every one of us. He has done so much for us that I can't even begin to express his value and contributions.

We would also like to dedicate this book to the thousands of loyal Nebraska fans who supported us through our entire careers. You have been patient and dedicated. The fans make Nebraska football memorable for all of us.

Finally, the 1995 Nebraska football seniors wish to dedicate this book to their respective families. Yes, we play the games for the fans! But above all, we dedicate the games to the ones we love, those who have provided unconditional support. Thank you and enjoy the book!

Aaron Graham, 1995 Nebraska Football Co-Captain

TABLE OF CONTENTS

FOREWORD

Behind Every Champion... is the story of a remarkable group of University of Nebraska senior football players. The great majority of this class entered school in the fall of 1991 and was not seen by most recruiting analysts as a particularly outstanding group of players. None of these so-called "experts" who rate recruiting classes believed that this was a group that even deserved to be mentioned among the elite recruiting classes in the country. However, these players were able to be part of five straight Big Eight Championships. Their won-lost record was 36-1 the last three years. They had three straight undefeated regular seasons and played in three national championship games. Each of the last two years they were undisputed national champions, having won 25 straight football games.

The most unusual thing about this group over the last two seasons was not the fact that they were undefeated or even that they had won two consecutive national championships — something that had not been done for many years. It was the fact that they were able to overcome so much adversity and still have success on the football field.

During the 1994 season our football team endured an unusual number of major injuries at key positions. It seemed that the more the injuries piled up, the more dedicated and determined this group of players became. They had a great will to succeed despite all odds.

The 1995 season, again, was played under great duress and was one in which we encountered a great deal of adversity. The problems that we encountered in 1995 were quite different from the 1994 season, however, in that the criticism and adversity that we endured came from outside of the program, primarily from the national media. The perception of our football team had generally been quite positive, and suddenly we were being portrayed as an "out of control" band of outlaws. Many teams would have come apart under the constant attacks, yet, again, this group seemed to only pull closer together, sharpen their focus, and become more committed to excellence on the football field.

The traits that these young men displayed to an exceptional degree had to do with heart, a strong work ethic, excellent leadership by example, exceptionally strong will to win, and above all, unity and caring for each other. In the case of this group, one might truly say that the whole was greater than the sum of its parts. They had fine individual talent, yet they were able to play as a team in a manner that exceeded the sum of their individual abilities.

The 1995 team was the best team that I have coached, and this group of seniors was the heart and soul of this team. Each season is a microcosm of life. Nearly all of the emotions that one experiences in a lifetime are packed into a season that spans only five months. The season tends to, at times, seem unbearably long and yet at other times goes by in a flash. In 1995 the highs and lows, the sorrow and despair, and the joy and satisfaction were unusually stark in their contrast and impact on all of us associated with the football team. The season was culminated by a surprisingly dominant performance in the national championship game in Tempe, Arizona, versus the University of Florida.

Just prior to that game, I held a short meeting with the senior players. I customarily have such a meeting with each group of seniors near the end of their final season. I told them how much I had appreciated their attitude, their confidence, and their ability to keep the team focused and on track. I had not anticipated their response, as there was a closeness and emotion that I had not experienced before in a meeting of this type. There were a few hugs, a few tears and a whole lot of commitment. When we left the room, I was certain that this group of seniors would see to it that our football team played at the very top of their abilities. I wasn't sure what the outcome of the game would be, but I knew that every ounce of energy that they were capable of generating would be laid on the line against Florida. Obviously their performance did not disappoint me or anyone on our coaching staff.

The ultimate measure of a team is quite likely not final with the last football game that they play but rather is determined over the next thirty to forty years. I would predict that this group of young men, collectively, will do very well. Attitude, dedication, work ethic, and willingness to be a contributor rather than a taker is everything, and they have all of these attributes in great abundance. I wish them well and hope that you enjoy gaining greater insight into this unique and remarkable group of individuals as you read each of their stories.

Dr. Tom Osborne
Head Football Coach
Nebraska Cornhuskers

PREFACE

The stories told in the following pages are reflections of the 1995 Nebraska football seniors. These twenty-one men have left their mark on Nebraska football history. As the writer for this book, it has been a great honor to have had the opportunity to get to know these football champions as individuals. Sometimes we forget that behind every champion is a person — a person really no different from you or me.

As you'll learn, the lives of many of these Nebraska football players can be likened to a roller coaster ride, full of ups and downs. Yes, these young men have known the exhilaration of winning, but they have also faced challenges, even tragedy. Some have lost parents. Others were raised without parents. Some have made mistakes and later had to deal with intense public scrutiny. In their personal stories, they speak of these events, and we learn how they went on to overcome the odds, to become champions.

In 1991, most national recruiting experts ranked this class, at best, as number thirty in the country. But the experts couldn't rank character, heart and desire. This group of young men exemplifies these traits to the highest degree. They never listened to the doubters, and in fact, many say they were inspired by their critics.

Within these pages, you'll also hear consistently that there is a leader behind every champion. To these seniors, that leader has been Head Nebraska Football Coach Tom Osborne, a man whom they credit for developing the person behind the player.

Finally, behind every champion...are great fans. Fans know the excitement of watching the Cornhuskers take the field. Now, learn what the view is like from the field, how players were moved to tears as they stepped before the roaring crowds at Memorial Stadium. These are just a few of the moments you'll share with the seniors of Nebraska's 1995 football team as they give you glimpses of their lives, of what made them champions.

Keith A. Zimmer

Keith A. Zimmer

Acknowledgments

As the writer for this book, I would like to thank the twenty-one Nebraska football seniors for sharing their personal stories for *Behind Every Champion....* I was deeply honored when the team captains asked that I help tell their stories. It was important for this group of seniors to express their feelings and reactions to one of the most memorable seasons ever in Nebraska football history.

A special thank you goes to Dr. Tom Osborne. We appreciate his leadership and ability to shape champions as well as his support for this project. Credit also goes to University of Nebraska-Lincoln administrators Bill Byrne, Al Papik and Dennis Leblanc for their help and enthusiasm.

I would also like to thank former Husker great and friend Trev Alberts for his support of *Behind Every Champion....* Alberts will forever be a part of the Nebraska football family.

Finally, a special word of thanks to my parents, Jerry and Helen and my brother, Nick for the lifetime of support they've provided me.

7

REGGIE BAUL

Speedster Reggie Baul of Bellevue, Nebraska, has always enjoyed athletics and the outdoors. Born in California, the son of James and Toni Baul, Reggie was afforded plenty of opportunities for recreation as a result of growing up on an Air Force base. "There were all kinds of leagues and chances to play with other kids and I really enjoyed that," recalled Baul. In the early years, Baul was fond of baseball, basketball and soccer. "I started at about age six or seven and had a blast just being outdoors and running off steam."

Baul's brother, Adrian who was twelve years older, was also active in sports, owing to the encouragement of his father. "My dad was involved with coaching my brother and maybe pushed him into sports too much. With me, I think he decided it would be better to be supportive but not be as involved. It was my decision to play and I determined the role athletics would play in my future," said Baul.

At age eight, Baul and his family moved from California to Nebraska. Reggie's father was stationed in Bellevue. Reggie continued to play sports, but didn't have a passion for football until the end of high school.

"Football seemed too structured for me. With sports like soccer and baseball, I could be more of an individual and not be so restricted," said Baul.

Baul didn't like restrictions. "Whenever I got grounded growing up, my punishment was to stay inside. Because of that, I always liked to do things outside," remembered Baul.

One thing Baul really liked was soccer. During his freshman year in high school at Papillion-LaVista, Baul played club soccer; he was also on the freshman football team. "Playing both sports was tiring and I think playing club soccer held back my development as a football player in the beginning," said Baul.

In the spring of 1988, soccer became a sanctioned high school sport and Baul was a legitimate two-sport athlete. "I remember after my sophomore year becoming really discouraged with football. I was almost ready to call it quits. After the junior varsity season, lots of the guys get moved up to varsity for the rest of the year, but I wasn't. I thought I should focus on soccer and from that point on thought I would go to college on a soccer scholarship," recalled Baul.

During the spring of his sophomore year, Baul was introduced to the head varsity football coach, Gene Suhr. "I liked his style and he said I should get involved with weight training and come out during my junior season." Reggie started liking football more, and heading into his senior year, he began to recognize he had a special gift. "Coach Suhr had a wide-open offense and it was really fun to be out there and be a go-to guy. If it wasn't for Coach Suhr and his approach to the game, I would have probably given up on football."

Despite a promising football future, Baul continued to play soccer in the spring. "I was All-State as a junior and colleges were beginning to recruit me as a soccer prospect. I was about to make an early commitment to accept a soccer scholarship to Creighton University when I began receiving some letters from Division II football coaches telling me I could play for their programs."

The letters of interest from various Division II football programs proved to be a critical turning point in Baul's athletic future. "Those letters told me that I had potential as a football player, so I decided to try to go out in style my senior year and get some interest from some big-time schools." Baul made good on his goal. In 1990, he lead Papillion-LaVista to the Class A football championship. The Super-State selection earned All-Nebraska honors for snaring 36 receptions for 812 yards and 12 touchdowns.

Suddenly, Division I programs, like Kansas, took notice of Baul. "I got a phone call from Kansas and then I started to get excited about football," said Baul. Shortly after the Jayhawks expressed interest in Baul, Nebraska, Colorado State and even Colorado began visiting with Baul. He liked the idea of being part of a tradition-rich football program. "I liked the atmosphere associated with college football. Everyone comes out for football games and it is fun to play in front of huge crowds. I think it brings out the best in me as an athlete."

Apparently Baul felt the Colorado State football program could help him develop even more. "I liked the wide-open offense and the fact that the coaches told me I could come in and play immediately," reflected Baul. As fate would have it, Baul never made it to Colorado State. In fact he did not see a football field in 1991 as a result of failing to meet NCAA initial-eligibility academic standards. "Once I found out I didn't qualify, I didn't want my family to be responsible for such expensive out-of-state tuition. That, along with the fact that Nebraska showed steady interest in me, made me decide to attend Nebraska as a freshman in 1991."

"I really liked the fact that Nebraska had a very structured academic support program. I knew I would need that throughout college; most other schools didn't seem nearly as concerned about the books as Nebraska," said Baul. He had not been without athletics since age seven, and now, in 1991, was sidelined from sports.

"Looking back on that year, I think sitting out was really good for me as a person and as a player. It helped me adjust to college and also made me want football even more," said Baul. He persisted through his Proposition 48 year and was confronted with a redshirt year in 1992. Again, Baul was able to find the silver lining in the redshirt season.

"In high school all I did was run and catch. Blocking at Nebraska was very important for the receivers so I guess the redshirt year was helpful. Still, it was really difficult because I had worked so hard to gain my eligibility. To sit out another year was a real test for me." Baul earned a scholarship in the spring of 1993, and with the guidance of mentor and college roommate Corey Dixon, he was more than ready for his coming out party during the 1993 season.

As a redshirt sophomore in 1993, Baul was ready to put on the Husker red and white. "I had been to Nebraska games before, so I didn't think taking the field for the first time would be that big of a deal. Some of the older guys like Trumane Bell and Corey Dixon were telling me I would be scared. Going out for warm-ups in front of half the crowd was what really made me nervous. I came onto the field with only about ten to twelve other receivers. So then, when I came out with the whole team in front of the sold-out stadium, I didn't feel quite as scared," remembered Baul.

Baul had an immediate impact with the Huskers in 1993 and along with starting split end Corey Dixon, the 5-8, 170-pounder was dubbed a part of the "itty bitty committee." Baul saw action in all eleven regular-season games, starting the UCLA game and the 1994 Orange Bowl. The bowl game proved to be especially memorable for Baul. He caught a tipped, 34-yard touchdown pass from Tommie Frazier in the second quarter to give the Huskers a 7-3 lead over top-ranked Florida State. "I was so focused on the game, I didn't realize what I had done. My intention was to help the team win the game, because nobody thought we had a prayer against Charlie Ward and Florida State," explained Baul.

As the game drew to a close, Baul experienced every human emotion possible. "I went through joy, anger, disbelief, disappointment and hope," said Baul. Even though the Huskers came up short on the score-board, Baul could tell the Huskers had special players with outstanding qualities.

"I could just tell that guys like Tommie Frazier, Aaron Graham, Clester Johnson, Lawrence Phillips and Christian Peter, to name a few, had that special desire to win. I knew that I wanted to 'go to war' with guys like that because they didn't want to come up short again," said Baul. As the future unfolded, Baul and the Huskers never came up short again on the gridiron.

In 1994, injuries and quarterback issues dominated the headlines on the Huskers' road to the promised land. "When Tommie got hurt, some of the guys were concerned about our chances to win it all. Not because we doubted Brook's ability, but because he had limited experience." According to Baul, Brook Berringer earned the team's respect because of his unselfish play. "He came in against Kansas State and basically just handed the ball off to the backs. You could tell it was important for him to be out there and I think his presence gave everyone a boost." The Huskers fought through the adversity in 1994 and made it through the regular sea-son unblemished, earning a return trip to the Orange Bowl. The Huskers once again had a chance at the national title — this time against the Miami Hurricanes.

Although the Huskers survived the 1994 season without a blemish, unfortunately the same was not true for Baul. Shortly before the end of the regular season, Baul was involved with an off-the-field incident. "I'm still mad because I allowed myself to be in a vulnerable position with the wrong crowd. Also, coming from Nebraska, I knew that if a player puts on the red and white he better be prepared for scrutiny. Still, I was 20 years old and I guess I didn't think it would become as big a deal as it did," said Baul. "I owe Coach Osborne a big apology. Even though he was a father-like figure, he was not my father and is not responsible for me. It wasn't fair the way others tried to bring him down. I also feel bad for my parents because they did a good job of teaching me right from wrong. I'm just going to have to live with what I did. People make mistakes and football players are people. I hope people don't label me and punish me forever."

The 1994 Huskers were labeled as the college football team with the most character and unity, who despite considerable odds, became national champions. "When we beat Miami, the whole team and even the entire nation seemed so happy for Coach Osborne," said Baul.

It was a long, hard journey to the top of college football. Nebraska coaches and players dedicated themselves to one goal for a complete year. In the end, the dream of being number one was realized. For as difficult as it was to get to the top, it didn't take long for critics to attempt to bring the Huskers down in 1995.

"I think I'm speaking for all of the players when I say that our hearts went out to Coach Osborne. He took the heat for off-field problems and it just didn't seem fair. One moment everyone loved the guy and the next moment people were questioning every move he made," said Baul. "Coach Osborne told the players and their families during recruiting that he would stand by each player from start to finish and he did. We all respect him for that. I respected the way he communicated with his players because he was very fair and soft-spoken." Baul and his Husker teammates were determined to use the criticism and scrutiny as incentive to repeat in 1995. "The 1995 National Championship was a family title. We all pulled together and did it for one another. As the season went on, we became more confident, determined and unified." The back-to-back national titles rank high on the list of Baul's Nebraska career reflections.

"I'm proud that I hung in there and didn't quit. I had some ups and downs during my years at Nebraska but I always faced things head on." Baul still has some unfinished business at Nebraska. "I really want to graduate. I feel like getting my diploma will be my third national championship. Many people said I couldn't graduate from college so that's always been a goal in the back of my mind," explained Baul.

As for his future, Baul said, "I want to own and operate my own club or radio station. I want to bring some added diversity to the Midwest and offer an atmosphere that reaches out to all types."

Without question, Reggie Baul has the ability to play football at the professional level. "Many people doubt that Nebraska receivers can play in the National Football League. Even though our receivers usually don't get the headlines, we are good athletes who perform well under pressure. When our number is called, we produce. I just hope I get the opportunity to display my talents," added Baul.

Reggie Baul learned valuable lessons in life. "My brother Adrian has helped teach me to not take things for granted and to make the most of every opportunity. Coach Osborne and his program helped me mature — from being a scared freshman to becoming a young man. I've always been able to find the good in the bad and I'm excited to begin the next chapter of my life."

8

TYRONE WILLIAMS

Tyrone Williams grew up in Palmetto, Florida, under the watchful eye of his grandmother, Louise Williams. "I left the hospital with my mother but was raised by my grandmother. I was with my mom for about one year and from that point on my grandmother has been the main person in my life," explained Williams. "My grandmother really cared and she was always getting me involved in sports to keep me out of trouble." As Williams remembers, he didn't have to look far to see trouble on a daily basis.

"Our duplex was in the worst part of town. Across the alley from our place was a night club and a bar. People would always park in the alley in case they had to make a quick getaway." Williams recalls always having their door open due to the heat in Florida. "People would come racing through our halls shooting and fighting all the time. I guess there were drug deals gone bad or something," said Williams. "I saw all kinds of things go down. I even saw a lady get shot in the head as she was running from the bar."

From the very onset of Williams' athletic career there was very little that went bad. "I started playing when I was nine or ten. I went out for all sports," explained Williams, although football was always the game he especially liked. "I was blessed with great speed and just always felt at ease on the field. I forgot all of the temptations to get into trouble when on the field."

In fact, as his athletic promise blossomed, the peer pressure to turn to crime diminished. "Once the dealers saw I had a good shot of making it and taking it to the next level, they pretty much left me alone. Sometimes they even tried to help me out."

Williams didn't need much extra help at Manatee High School. "I felt lucky to go to a high school with one of the top football programs in the nation. It was like college because we had two-a-days, spring ball and winter conditioning. Our school did things most other programs didn't think about or have the funds to do." The extra effort paid big dividends for both Manatee High School and Williams. He sparkled at I-back and defensive back, helping his team to a 12-1 record in 1991. The quarterback for Manatee was future Husker star Tommie Frazier.

"The thing I remember most about my high school career was that I loved playing in big-time pressure games. I seemed to always do my best under those circumstances," recalled Williams. Williams was ready to excel in college football when he discovered he did not meet the minimum NCAA initial eligibility academic standards.

Williams ultimately decided to attend Nebraska primarily because of the supportive academic environment for Husker athletes. "I felt Nebraska was the best place for me as a student and an athlete," remarked Williams. Comfortable with his decision to attend Nebraska along with his high school teammate Tommie Frazier, Williams still struggled with the adjustment to Nebraska's capital city.

"It was a new experience for me. In the past, when football season came around, I would play. Now I couldn't. At first I thought it would be no problem, but as time went on it got more and more difficult." The difficulty in transition for Williams was compounded because of the lifestyle differences between Florida and Nebraska. "Things seemed much slower and relaxed in Nebraska. I'm not saying that was bad, only that it was different and took time getting used to."

After sitting out his first year in Lincoln, Williams was primed for the 1993 season. As a first-year sophomore, Williams got an early chance to display his ability. "I was just hoping to play some special teams and maybe make the travel squad. I was surprised when I got quite a bit of playing time in our third game," said Williams. The coaches apparently saw enough of Williams to know they had a special player. Williams started the next game and never relinquished his starting role the remainder of his career.

"I wasn't sure if I would be able to learn the defense in such a short time. It seemed like I was studying film all the time. But I really prepared hard and I think that showed on the field." Williams started seven of the Huskers' last eight games at right corner and had earned Big Eight Co-Defensive Newcomer-of-the-Year honors by season's end. "It was a great honor to win that award, especially when you consider what some of the previous winners have gone on to accomplish. Nebraska players like Bruce Pickens and Trev Alberts went on to be high NFL draft picks."

Williams had the chance to play against some of the game's best athletes in the 1994 Orange Bowl against top-ranked Florida State. "It was a fun game with loads of pressure, but I wouldn't have wanted it any other way. Everything about the game was electrifying, including all of the Florida State receivers. Everybody was saying it would be a track meet for their receivers." Williams and the Husker blackshirt defenders held Heisman Trophy winner Charlie Ward and a potent offense in check. Williams recorded a career high nine tackles — eight solo — with three pass breakups.

"Even though we lost the game, our team showed the heart and desire to win. It was a great learning experience for the whole team," remembered Williams.

Upon returning home to Palmetto, Florida, after the defeat, Williams was heckled by some of his hometown boys. "People were telling me that I should have gone to a Florida school and that Nebraska could never win

the big games. I told them that the championship would
be ours next year and left it at that." All things considered it was quite a successful first year of college football for Williams.

Williams experienced similar success in the classroom. "The biggest thing about college is time manage-
ment. Once I learned how to set priorities and use my
time wisely, I felt like college was a place where I fit
in. It was important for me to do well in school because
I knew people labeled me as an academic risk." Just as
Williams was determined to win in the classroom, his
Husker teammates were determined to win in 1994.

"From the moment we left the hotel in Miami after
the Florida State loss, we just knew we weren't going to
be denied. Nothing was going to get in our way." It
wasn't all smooth sailing for the Huskers. The team had
to overcome the loss of starting quarterback Tommie
Frazier to blood clots. "At first, I thought somebody was
going to have to really step up or we were going
down." For Williams it was hard to see best friend and
high school teammate Frazier be sidelined with an injury. "It hurt to see him in the hospital bed with a
problem he couldn't control. Tommie is such a competitor that I figured he would be back to play a big
role for the team somewhere down the line. The thing
about Tommie that is so special is the size of his heart.
Succeeding was very important to him," said Williams.

Success was also important to Williams. "In looking
back, I think it was our defense that stepped it up a
notch during Tommie's absence. Our feeling was if the

offense scored three points, we would win the game," explained Williams. The Huskers rose above the adversity, won 12 regular season games and were back in the national championship game in the 1995 Orange Bowl against the hometown Miami Hurricanes. And just as Williams had predicted, Tommie Frazier opened the game as starter before giving way to Brook Berringer in the second and third quarters. Frazier came up huge in the fourth quarter, rallying the Huskers to a come-from-behind 24-17 victory and a national championship.

"Coach Osborne just told us to play hard for 60 minutes and to always keep our poise. He said that sooner or later we would wear them down and win the game. That's exactly how it happened," recalled Williams. "The win was very emotional for me. To beat Miami in the Orange Bowl for the big prize definitely gave me the bragging rights when I returned home." More than anything, Williams was happy for his head coach, Dr. Tom Osborne. "I was so happy for him and the other coaches. I know he would still say it was 'no big deal' to this day. That title was dedicated to Coach Osborne from our team and all of the past players who ever played for the man."

Williams had more than made up for the disappointment of missing the 1992 season. Two seasons of football and two national championship games with one title: Could things get any better for Williams and the Huskers? "We definitely felt the talk of a repeat was legitimate," Williams said. "After I saw some people erase doubts during spring ball and fill some gaps, I knew then that we had a great chance of doing it again," remembered Williams.

It seemed the Huskers' chances of going back-to-back might take a huge step backward with some off-the-field incidents which received national media attention. "All I can say is we must have had the best team in 1995, because everyone was doing their best to tear us down to the bottom. Everyone wanted to be a critic and make up stories from bits and pieces of information. I don't think people should make quick judgments until they know the whole situation."

In the midst of the 1995 scrutiny, past isolated incidents resurfaced including one involving Tyrone Williams. "I really don't want to get into specifics. I'm sure some people label me as a criminal and that is their choice. I can't worry about what others think. Most people don't know or understand my background." Williams describes himself as a "laid back, quiet person who doesn't seek attention." "If one positive came out of the situation, I learned how to meet adversity head on and not run from it. I just want people to know that one incident shouldn't define character. I'd never gotten into any trouble prior to 1994; I want to express my regrets to my family. I felt so ashamed at the time," recalled Williams.

Williams credits Coach Tom Osborne for his loyalty to the players. "You expect to have a foundation of people who care for you and support you at all times. Family, friends and people like Coach Osborne gave me the comfort and help I really needed. Coach Osborne was always willing to step in and take the heat to defend his players, just like he had always promised he would do if needed," said Williams.

Williams and the Huskers were inspired to play unified football through the 1995 season. "I wanted to go out and play my heart out for Coach Osborne. When you get 150 players unified, striving for one goal, it can be pretty powerful." The Huskers proved themselves by capping another perfect season to repeat as national champions in the 1996 Fiesta Bowl. "The '95 team should be remembered as a very special group. I think our team redefined the words character and unity," said Williams.

Tyrone Williams is a young man who has come a long way since arriving in Nebraska in 1992. "I've been through lots of ups and downs. I feel like I've become a man during my time at Nebraska. I'm proud of the way I've handled things, both the good and the bad."

"I know college graduation will be the most memorable moment of my life without a doubt. I am happy that my grandmother will be there to share the day. The diploma will be for her," said Williams. It is important for Williams to remember his roots and those who have been role models in his life. "My grand-mother has been my top role model. She gave me direction in life and made sacrifices to give me a chance. Tom Osborne is my other role model. I never had any male figures growing up and he is one man who has supported me like a father. I will forever be a Tom Osborne and Nebraska fan."

As for his future, Williams says, "I think it looks really good for me in the National Football League. It's been a dream of mine since playing Pop Warner ball. Whenever playing football comes to an end, I want to go back to Florida and work with troubled teens. I think they need help getting ready for college. It's important for me to give back to the community and to the kids," said Williams. Williams has several messages to stress. "Almost everyone makes mistakes in their life. You can regret it, but you can't change it. Just always try to make good decisions and rely on those who are close to you."

9
TONY VELAND

If any athlete is truly deserving of the nickname "Captain Comeback," it would be Nebraska co-captain Tony Veland. Unlike Indianapolis Colts quarterback Jim Harbaugh who earned the same nickname for his dramatic fourth quarter comebacks, Veland's nickname rings true in all aspects. The first half of Veland's Nebraska career was riddled with injury, causing him at times to contemplate his football future. "Hanging up my cleats was a distant thought but it definitely was something I considered," said the Omaha Benson High School graduate. Fortunately, Veland stuck with the game and concluded his Husker campaign in glorious fashion as a team co-captain and starter for the blackshirts.

Veland's decision to become a Cornhusker was finalized during the summer of his junior year in high school, when he attended Big Red Football Camp. "That is where I proved myself as an athlete and is when the coaches told me they would offer me a scholarship." A highly-touted high school quarterback, Veland became the recruitment target of numerous schools including Iowa State, Kansas State and Colorado. In the end, several factors convinced Veland it was in his best interest to stay home. "Nebraska showed interest in me early on and was really the first Division I school to look at me as a scholarship prospect. Coach Osborne struck me as a man who would be very fair and committed to his players off the field."

Recruited as a quarterback and defensive back, Veland redshirted in 1991, which proved helpful in his adjustment to the quarterback position. Veland was progressing at a rapid pace when in 1992, as a redshirt freshman, he earned the number one quarterback spot during spring drills after senior Mike Grant suffered a broken collarbone. Veland's first confrontation with adversity soon followed; during a controlled scrimmage just before the start of the 1992 campaign, he also was sidelined with a broken collarbone. The injury resulted in Veland missing the first five games and then being relegated to the role of third string quarterback behind Tommie Frazier and Mike Grant.

After seeing action in only four games in 1992, Veland was determined to battle for the quarterback spotlight in 1993. Solidifying himself in the number two quarterback slot behind Tommie Frazier, misfortune was again just around the corner for Veland. In the second game of the season against North Texas State, Veland tore his right patellar tendon and ended up playing in only two games during his sophomore season. "That was the low point of my Nebraska career. It was like the Lord was sending me a message to get out of the game."

Two seasons of eligibility for Tony Veland had brought two major football injuries. Many would have been completely devastated by the injuries, but Veland didn't lose faith. "The injuries helped me mature and made me realize I was not invincible — like I thought I was in high school. I also became more determined to develop other aspects of my life and work hard to be a total person." Veland credits his spirituality and the support from family and friends as critical to helping him through his down times. "In the end, it was my competitive nature that kept me from giving up on football," said Veland.

After grueling rehabilitation on his knee and repeated setbacks during his first three years at Nebraska, Tony Veland felt it was time for a position change. "Actually, while I was in the hospital with the knee injury, I contemplated the position change. I had repeated bad breaks at quarterback and felt I was a good enough all-around athlete to make the transition to the defensive backfield. Frazier had proved himself as quarterback and it was important for me to have the chance to play, especially if I was going to be motivated to work hard during rehab."

It will come as no surprise to those who know Tony Veland that he dedicated himself to excellence during his rehabilitation and was approaching the 1994 Husker football campaign close to complete recovery. Despite missing all of spring drills, Veland was a quick study at free safety. "I think my intelligence and athleticism really helped me make a fast adjustment," recalled Veland. As fate would have it, the conversion from quarterback to defensive back proved to be a blessing in disguise. He saw his first action in the Husker secondary during the 1994 Kickoff Classic rout of West Virginia — Veland's coming out party in the secondary. "I had so much energy built up in me. I guess I let it all out on the field." Veland proved to the nation he had the ability to play defense by recording some of the games' biggest hits. "I wanted to prove to myself and my teammates that I could play the position," remarked Veland.

During Nebraska's next game against Texas Tech on national television, Veland was called upon to see if he was worthy of a blackshirt. Starting free safety Mike Minter suffered a torn anterior cruciate ligament, meaning Veland and Eric Stokes would have to step up their play to help the Huskers reach their goal — a national championship.

Veland started ten games during the 1994 season despite playing at less than 100 percent as a result of his injury. Midway through the Huskers' national championship drive, the Huskers experienced major quarterback woes when quarterbacks Tommie Frazier and Brook Berringer were injured. "There was a furious scramble for able quarterbacks and the staff approached me about switching. I felt I worked so hard to make the change to safety and with the injury to Minter, it was important that I stay in the secondary," concluded Veland. He and the Huskers overcame their injuries to finish a perfect 12-0 and earn a berth in their second consecutive national championship game.

January 1, 1995...the day the Huskers and the Nebraska faithful had been waiting for since Nebraska's heartbreaking loss against Florida State in 1994. "Our team was focused to 'finish business' and win the Orange Bowl. We especially wanted to do it for Coach Osborne. We were getting tired of hearing the same old talk that we couldn't win a big game or defend a passing team. People were counting us out before we even played the game." Nebraska's dramatic 24-17 win against Miami didn't seem real until Kareem Moss intercepted Frank Costa's pass. "When Kareem picked off that pass, I let out a big sigh of relief and became really emotional. Everyone was excited to get the monkey off Coach Osborne's back."

Veland is a firm believer that good things come to those who work hard and persevere and good things continued to happen for Veland. Prior to the start of the 1995 season, Veland was elected as one of five senior co-captains. "In the beginning, I was surprised by the announcement, but after thinking it through I can see why the team voted me as captain. I carry myself in a respectable manner and make an effort to get along with everyone." Indeed, Veland has always been considered a positive role model to the youth throughout Nebraska. His leadership qualities and those of the other Husker captains were put to a stern test as a result of a few highly publicized, off-the-field incidents.

Despite the national scrutiny and determined efforts by some to ridicule the Nebraska program, Veland knew the team would overcome the negative publicity. "There were no problems within the team or among individuals, rather a few guys made wrong decisions. Our coach and our team decided not to give up on those guys and tried to bond closer together as a team."

As a senior, Veland started every game and earned second-team All-Big Eight honors in both the AP and Coaches' Polls. Veland was also successful on the football field. He was elected captain by his teammates for his senior year. "The captain role was a new challenge and I decided to hit it head on. Everyone knows I'm usually a soft-spoken guy who doesn't say much." Veland let his actions on the field do most of his talking. He finished the 1995 season seventh on the team with 38 tackles, 22 of which were solo.

For the most part, Veland was quiet in the locker room before games. But prior to Nebraska departing for the national championship clash with Florida in the 1996 Fiesta Bowl, Veland inspired the team with powerful words shown to the team on video. Veland's message: "Everyone is talking about Florida, Wuerffel and the fun & gun. I'm tired of hearing about the Gators. We have the best team in the nation." Veland went on to list each position emphasizing the fact that Nebraska had the best quarterback, the best offensive line, the most aggressive linebackers, a great secondary and the finest coaching staff in the country.

The inspirational message helped propel the Huskers to a dominating 62-24 victory over Florida. "The Fiesta Bowl win and the second title didn't hit me until I got back to Lincoln and caught up on some rest. The five straight Big Eight titles and back-to-back national championships made me realize we would be remembered as one of the best college football teams ever."

Veland was especially proud of the job done by the 1995 team captains. "It was a heck of a year to be a captain. We had a great blend of people who helped the team overcome the scrutiny and adversity. It was as though this team conquered the world," said Veland.

Veland will also forever remember the last time he entered Memorial Stadium on November 24th for the game against Oklahoma. "I was very sentimental. I tried to pay close attention to all the details — the crowd, the noise, the weather. I was determined to stay focused on the game and still have a memorable home finale." Veland came up huge against the Sooners in the last-ever Big Eight Conference game. Veland picked up a fumble and raced 57 yards for a touchdown, helping the Huskers clinch a spot in the Fiesta Bowl.

Tony Veland, Nebraska's version of "Captain Comeback," is pleased with his Nebraska football experience. "At times it felt like 'me against all the odds.' I believe I showed lots of character in this program and made the most of my chances. It's time for me to step aside as a Husker and let someone else take over. I will always be a diehard Nebraska fan."

An exceptional athlete, Veland has the ability to play at the next level, but isn't banking on it. "I'm a realist and will give professional football my best shot. I won't be devastated if I don't make it."

With or without football, Veland has a bright future. He will likely pursue a graduate degree in engineering before testing the job market.

15

TOMMIE FRAZIER

Husker quarterback Tommie Frazier has forever earned his place in Nebraska football history. The first true freshman to start at quarterback for the Big Red since 1985, Frazier has permanently etched his name in the record books. Frazier owns Nebraska career records for total offense with 5,476 yards and touchdowns with 79. The Husker faithful will not soon forget the individual and team contributions of the first-team consensus 1995 All-American. According to Frazier, the recipe for his success both on and off the field involved one key ingredient. "I have always been a very determined person. For as long as I can remember, I have had a history of proving people wrong."

Back in Bradenton, Florida, Frazier grew up wanting to be a running back. At age seven, during little league practice, a defining moment occurred for Frazier. "My cousin was the coach and he told me to throw the football. I threw it farther than anyone on the team and from that day on I have always been a quarterback," recalled Frazier. The son of Tommie and Priscilla Frazier, Tommie developed rapidly as an athlete and won the starting quarterback position at Manatee High School during his junior season. In two seasons, Frazier passed for 2,600 yards and 30 touchdowns while rushing for over 1,600 yards and 33 touchdowns. He earned *USA Today* All-American recognition.

Coming out of a powerhouse high school football program and posting impressive statistics, Frazier soon had the attention of recruiters nationwide. "My mother was very involved in the recruitment process. We would listen to the presentation of every coach. My mother is a very good judge of character and honesty. She could usually tell an honest person from one who wasn't," recalled Frazier. Frazier's father tried to stay out of the decision process. "He knew in order for me to become a man, I would have to be able to sort through everything and make important decisions on my own."

Frazier didn't have to sort through much correspondence from the major Florida football schools like Miami, Florida and Florida State. "They wrote me one or two times but never really showed serious interest in me. Apparently they didn't think I could play quarterback. From that point on, I knew I would be leaving the state and would prove I could play college quarterback at a major school."

Several factors influenced Frazier's decision-making. "I didn't want a team to change my position and I didn't want to be told up front that I would redshirt. I just wanted a chance to see if I could play right away." On the semi-short list for Frazier were Colorado, Clemson, Syracuse, Notre Dame, Georgia Tech, Washington, Tennessee and Nebraska. After taking official visits to Colorado, Clemson, Syracuse and Notre Dame, Frazier prepared to commit to Notre Dame until mother Priscilla stepped in. "She reminded me that I had made a commitment to at least visit Nebraska and that I should honor what I told the Nebraska coaches." Frazier followed up with a campus visit to Lincoln. "I really liked what I saw at Nebraska. They had the best balance of winning football tradition and academic support. Also, I liked the fact that Coach Osborne said I would have a chance to play as a true freshman and would remain at quarterback for my career," recalled Frazier.

Frazier had considered making an early announcement prior to the national letter-of-intent signing date but felt it would be better to wait until signing day. "I felt if I committed early, the other schools would continue to pressure me and attempt to get me to change my mind," said Frazier. On signing day, a brief but very important press conference was scheduled at Manatee High School. "I had told nobody where I was going. My family, high school coaches and college coaches had no idea. I liked the suspense and drama. I walked up to the microphone and announced that I would be playing college football at the University of Nebraska. I looked at my Mom and she was crying. Her reaction told me that I had made the best decision. I was very relieved the decision was made. From there on, it was up to me to make it work for the best," said Frazier.

Even though he had a positive outlook, Frazier's transition to campus life was less than smooth. "I was very nervous coming to a place that was fifteen hundred miles from home. I was only seventeen years old and I was sad to leave my family for the first time. I had no idea what to expect." Upon arriving, Frazier was lonely and kept to himself. He credits former Nebraska assistant coach, Kevin Steele, as being very helpful. "He was supportive and a good guy to talk to. I got to know him throughout the recruitment process and felt comfortable going to him."

Then Frazier feared a sudden illness might hurt his chances for seeing action on the field. "I came down with a stomach virus and missed nearly all of two-a-days. I lost fifteen pounds in three days. It was a real setback for me but I wasn't going to give up on my goal — playing as a freshman." Frazier spent countless hours studying film and the playbook with quarterback coach Turner Gill. "Suddenly all of the hard work seemed to be paying off. I felt I was picking up the offense and maybe had a chance to play. Throw in a couple of injuries to guys ahead of me, including Mike Grant, and I got my chance," said Frazier.

Frazier made the most of his chance, starting in the Huskers' fourth game of the season against Missouri in the 1992 season. "I was really scared and wondered how the older guys would react to me. They could see in my eyes that I was nervous, but they all got behind me. A couple of times in the huddle I called the plays wrong and everyone just told me to calm down and think about things for a couple of seconds. I guess I just needed their support and vote of confidence." It didn't take long for Frazier to gain the respect of his elder players. Frazier fueled a fourth quarter surge to lead Nebraska to a 34-24 win in Columbia. Frazier's impressive debut was a sign of great things to come. He rushed for 77 yards and three scores and was 9 for 20 through the air with 157 yards and zero turnovers. "All things considered I felt pretty good and knew I would improve with each week."

Frazier indeed matured with each passing week. And although the team stumbled in Ames, Iowa, against Iowa State, Frazier gained national attention and recognition for his command of the Nebraska Cornhuskers. Frazier was the unanimous Big Eight Offensive Newcomer/Freshman-of-the-Year named by both the AP and Coaches, earned second-team freshman All-American honors for *Football News* and was an honorable-mention AP All-Big Eight pick. Of greater importance to Frazier was the chance to return to Florida and play in the Orange Bowl against Florida State. "It was neat to go back home so soon and show people that I could be quarterback for a big-time program. I felt I played all right, but I had two turnovers that cost us dearly," remembered Frazier. Nebraska lost the 1993 Orange Bowl, 27-14.

Frazier completed his rookie season with five wins, two losses and several important lessons learned. "I discovered that hard work and dedication pays off. If you put your mind to something, your goals can become realized. Despite losing the bowl game, I was really excited for my second year because I knew I would continue to get a better grasp of the offense."

With Frazier's early success came a loss of privacy. "The recognition came quickly and it seemed that I couldn't go anywhere without being noticed. At times I would stay in my dorm room, but I didn't like doing that," said Frazier. Under the right circumstances, Frazier enjoyed being a celebrity sports figure. "I enjoy the attention up to a point. If I'm out eating with my friends or out watching a basketball game, then that is my time. I think it's disrespectful to constantly be interrupted and asked for autographs and pictures. I just feel there is a proper time and place for it and that's when I enjoy doing it."

Frazier's star-like status escalated in coming years during one of the most celebrated Nebraska careers in recent memory. In 1993, Frazier added to his legacy by engineering several come-from-behind victories. He also led the Huskers to an 11-0 perfect regular season earning Nebraska an invitation to the national championship game against Florida State in the 1994 Orange Bowl.

"I really wanted that game because I felt like I didn't play up to my potential in the previous bowl game. I wanted to prove to the nation that I was a good quarterback and our team wanted to earn the respect of the country. We felt like we had nothing to lose since we were 17-point underdogs." In fact, most of the national media resorted to focusing on matchups within the game since most believed the Huskers were not in the same league as Florida State. "Many people were comparing me to Heisman Trophy winner Charlie Ward. He's a great competitor but the game was Nebraska against Florida State and not Frazier versus Ward."

Frazier and Ward played to a draw, both totaling 283 total yards in offense; however, the Seminoles walked away with an 18-16 victory and a national championship. "Looking back on that game, I think when we took the lead with 1:16 left, we celebrated too early and had somewhat of a letdown. Still, I thought there was plenty of time to get in field goal range. We did all of that but I guess it just wasn't meant to be." The fact that Frazier was named Most Valuable Player did little to offset his overall disappointment.

"I saw lots of disappointment and anger in the locker room. A couple of calls here and there could have changed the whole outcome of the game. We took ownership for losing the lead and decided to take matters into our own hands from that moment on. We decided in the locker room that we would be back and win it the following year," remembered Frazier.

Like his team members, Frazier places high value on his relationship with Coach Tom Osborne. "During my freshman year, I was so young and just didn't feel comfortable talking with him. Gradually, I became more and more relaxed around him. Eventually, we would start to joke with one another. We could make one another laugh which made for a better football relationship," explained Frazier. "As time went on, we could look at one another and almost sense what the other was thinking. I think I became an extension of him on the field and sometimes off the field."

By 1994, Frazier, a junior, entered the season a Davey O'Brien and Heisman favorite. Frazier and the Huskers made impressive opening game statements in the Kickoff Classic against West Virginia. The Huskers won 31-0 and Frazier collected yet another Most Valuable Player trophy. The Huskers were rolling and off to a 4-0 start. But then Frazier was sidelined with blood clots prior to the Wyoming game.

"I was devastated because I didn't understand what caused the blood clots and why this was happening to me. I saw my career flash in front of me and most of the experts wrote me off for good," recalled Frazier. "It was a roller coaster ride. One minute I was being told there was no chance I would play again and then I was told I might be able to play. Emotionally, I lost my energy and enthusiasm. It was a very draining process for me and my family."

In early October 1994, Frazier had surgery to tie off a small superficial vein in his lower calf, which contained a small clot that might have produced more significant clotting. "I didn't understand everything they were doing. All I knew was that being away from football was really tough on me. It got to the point where I didn't want to be around the team or the stadium. I told Coach Osborne that it was just too hard for me to sit in meetings knowing I wasn't going to play. He understood my competitiveness and was very supportive," said Frazier.

Without football for the first time in his life since age seven, Frazier channeled his energies toward school. "I threw myself into the books and really started to zero in on the goal of earning my degree." Frazier expanded his friendships off the football field. He also relied upon the support of his family. "My mom came to visit quite a bit and my brother had moved in with me the previous year. Their support got me through lots of tough moments."

In Frazier's absence, junior quarterback Brook Berringer proved to be a very capable player. "Sure, it was tough for me to watch Brook. I was happy that he was able to keep the team going and stay on track to reach all of our pre-season goals." Later, the national media attempted to build controversy between Frazier and Berringer. "It's not realistic to think you are going to have a great friendship with every player on the team. Brook and I came from different walks of life and we had very different interests. When it came to football, we supported one another. I rooted for him and did what I could to help him out on the field," explained Frazier.

After being denied a medical redshirt year by the National Collegiate Athletic Association (NCAA), Frazier was cleared for non-contact practice in mid-November. He was a late addition to the travel roster for the Nebraska at Oklahoma game. "I knew I was an emergency quarterback and would play only if Brook or Matt Turman got injured. It was still very positive for me. Being able to be a part of the team and travel with them was healthy for my emotional well-being and confidence," said Frazier.

Following Nebraska's victory at Oklahoma, Frazier was back on blood-thinners and continued non-contact practice until the final scrimmage in Miami prior to the '95 Orange Bowl. Slowly but surely, Frazier's confidence was returning. "I knew I could become the starter again. I wanted to perform like I did at the beginning of the year." In a difficult decision, Coach Tom Osborne gave the starting nod to Frazier for the '95 Orange Bowl against Miami. "It didn't make much difference to me who started the game. Brook and I both knew we'd play equal amounts. I was pleased to get the start but my main thing was to try and be the guy on the field at the end of the game."

Both Frazier and Berringer had their moments during the 1995 national championship tilt with Miami. Frazier re-entered the game at the start of the fourth quarter with the Huskers behind the Hurricanes. "It was one of those things where I could sense I needed to do something to boost the team and recharge them. I gave them a few words of encouragement and this time looked at them with confidence in my eyes and told them good things were going to happen." On a crucial third and four, Frazier ripped a 25-yard run on the option to set up Cory Schlesinger's game-winning touchdown. "With that run, I felt I was finally the Tommie Frazier of old. I felt smooth. I believe that run fired up the offense and the defense," remarked Frazier.

Nebraska held on to a dramatic 24-17 victory. "At the time, I couldn't sort everything out. I was just happy to help the team win and be a part of Coach Osborne's first national title. Words can't express how the team felt for Coach Osborne." While the Husker team was accepting the national championship trophy, Frazier was somewhat reluctant to walk away with his second consecutive Orange Bowl Most Valuable Player award. "I had no control over who the media gave those awards to. I tried to be humble with those honors and give credit where credit is due. Individual awards aren't that meaningful because football is a team sport," said Frazier.

It had been quite a junior season for Tommie Frazier. The comeback was complete and the team goal realized. Certainly, Frazier had plenty to celebrate after walking away from the Orange Bowl on New Year's Day, 1995. "I remember being on the bus after the game going back to the hotel. Coach Osborne and I were sitting up front and we made eye contact, smiled at one another and then started to eat our sandwiches. No words were needed. We knew what the other was thinking and how happy we were for one another."

Even though the unassuming Frazier shrugs at the label, by 1995 he had achieved celebrity-like status in the Cornhusker state. Frazier had always tried to remain the person behind the champion, especially among the Nebraska faithful. "I knew early on in my career that many kids were picking me as their role model. Even though I don't think all athletes make the best role models, I've always tried to show the kids that I do care about them and was willing to help youth make tough life-decisions." Frazier frequently visited terminally-ill children and accident victims in hospitals in an effort to provide encouragement and hope.

Hope and optimism ran high for Frazier and the Huskers in 1995. While the Huskers and Dr. Tom Osborne were prepared to defend the title, Frazier was once again being touted as one of college football's premiere players. "My major goal was to prove to the country that I was a complete quarterback. It was important for me not to be labeled exclusively as an option quarterback and let people know I was an efficient passer."

One title Frazier didn't receive at the beginning of the '95 campaign was that of team captain. "Even though I wasn't elected a team captain, I knew I was a team leader on the field. Other than the first few games of my career, I have always felt like a captain and I think my teammates and coaches would agree. I remember Coach Osborne coming up to me after the election of captains. He told me that he felt bad that I had not been elected a captain. I told him there was no need to feel that way because I understood my role and importance to the team."

Arguably, Frazier had become one of the most important cogs in the Big Red machine. Once again and true to form, Frazier proved to be a difference-

maker in 1995. One of Frazier's many shining moments came at Folsom Field in Boulder, Colorado. He
proved to be more than a complete player as he
passed for a career-high 241 yards and rushed for
another 40 while directing a penalty-free game. The
44-21 victory was highlighted by a second quarter play
in which Frazier withstood a fierce hit from a Colorado
defender and still managed to complete a 35-yard pass
to Ahman Green.

Frazier was living up to the Heisman hype and
enjoying a productive year on the field. But his
achievements and those of his teammates often took a
back seat to heavy negative national media coverage
of isolated off-the-field incidents involving several
players, some of which happened two to three years
before. "It was hard to deal with all of the distractions
in the beginning because we were really rolling. Later
everyone expressed his feelings, and we came up with
a new, more determined attitude," explained Frazier.

"People make mistakes and wrong decisions everyday. Nebraska football players are human beings.
Maybe some of the mistakes could have been avoided.
Still, we can't lose faith in a person because of a
mistake. The bottom line is people must learn from
their mistakes," said Frazier. As a team, Frazier and the
Huskers exemplified character and unity and marched
on to their third consecutive undefeated season and
national championship game. Before the Huskers
would clash with the Florida Gators in the 1996 Fiesta
Bowl, Frazier was anxious to bring closure to some of
the many individual awards he had been nominated

for. "At times all of the awards started to distract me on the field and I had to refocus so I didn't lose sight of the more important team goals," remarked Frazier.

Tommie Frazier collected his share of hardware in his senior season. Frazier won the Johnny Unitas Golden Arm Award and was a consensus All-American quarterback. Frazier came up just short in his bid to become Nebraska's third Heisman Trophy winner — runner-up to winner Eddie George of Ohio State. "The Heisman was never in the back of my mind. I knew from the very beginning I had no control over that award or any others. The one thing I knew I could control was helping lead our team to another title. I'd rather have a championship trophy and ring over the Heisman any day," Frazier said.

Finally, Nebraska was scheduled to play the last college football game of the 1995 season on January 2nd, 1996; Frazier had the opportunity to leave a lasting impression. "It was important for the team to play well to show our resolve after all the adversity we were faced with. Also, it was important for me to have a good game in hopes of being remembered as one of the best college football players in the country," said Frazier.

Frazier and his teammates were confident leading up to the 1996 Fiesta Bowl. "Everyone was bragging up Florida's offense. Yes, they were good, but I didn't feel they played a defense as quick or physical as ours was. If we executed the game plan, I thought we could dominate."

Frazier concluded his Nebraska career much the same way he started in 1992 in Columbia, Missouri. It was one big play after another on the road to claiming back-to-back national championships. Frazier rushed for 199 yards and passed for an additional 105 yards while figuring in three scores. Frazier showcased the leadership, resiliency and drama that Husker fans had come to expect. Some even say Frazier upstaged the 1971 Johnny "The Jet" Rodgers' 72-yard punt return against Oklahoma in the "Game-of-the-Century." Frazier lived up to his reputation as one of the best big-time gamers in college football with a "determined" 75-yard touchdown run. On his way to the end zone Frazier broke seven tackles and dragged several defenders before breaking free down the sideline. According to Frazier, the play was just another play. "I don't rank my runs. All of my plays are special to me. It was just a guy determined not to be tackled or not to fumble the football. ESPN and the ESPY awards later voted Frazier's memorable run as the 1995 College Football Play-of-the-Year.

Frazier is the ultimate team player, but he attempts to downplay some of his many defining moments. "Yes, I was happy with my performance but I was more satisfied for the team and for Coach Tom Osborne to go out on top. I guess I couldn't have scripted a better game and a better way to close out my college career," Frazier said.

Frazier is leaving Nebraska with four Big Eight conference championship rings, two national championship rings and a host of other trophies, but his biggest prize is his college diploma. "The college diploma means more to me than all of my team and individual accomplishments. The degree means a great deal to me and my parents," said the communication studies major. "Nobody can take education away from you. I've learned that football is very fragile. Maybe I played my last down of football in the Fiesta Bowl. I hope not, but the insecurity of football and injury factors are reasons I've been so intense about college graduation."

Odds are Tommie Frazier will take his considerable football talents to the professional ranks. "I've always dreamed of being a pro quarterback. Some say I'm not big enough or that blacks don't ever make it as a pro-style quarterback. I don't buy any of that. The way I see it, if a guy has good leadership skills and can win football games, he can be a pro quarterback. I've proven that in high school and in college. I'm hoping for the opportunity to do the same in the National Football League," explained Frazier.

How does Tommie want to be remembered as a Cornhusker? "I want to be remembered as a student who graduated on time and as a player who competed hard and gave 100 percent at all times. As a person, I want people to remember me as a very sincere young man with genuine qualities," said Frazier. "I have enjoyed the Nebraska experience tremendously. I would make the same decision all over again. I couldn't have asked for anything more."

Tommie Frazier has truly left his mark in Husker history and he has his photo on magazine covers to prove it. Still, he remains humble. "I'm flattered by all of the compliments but it's all just a matter of determination. I was determined to play quarterback and especially to play again after the blood clots. Determination can take a guy a long way and I will rely upon that trait every day for the rest of my life."

Brook Beringer

18

BROOK BERRINGER

The word "character" truly exemplifies Husker quarterback Brook Berringer. Like several other Husker senior teammates, Berringer had to overcome a family tragedy at an early age and repeatedly prove his ability to play football. The eventual roller coaster football ride Berringer embarked upon at the University of Nebraska-Lincoln pales in comparison to the crisis he and his family endured when Brook was in the second grade.

Born in Scottsbluff, Nebraska, Berringer and his two sisters Nicoel and Drue were raised by Warren and Jan Berringer in Goodland, Kansas. Warren Berringer was a dedicated father and also had a passion for the great outdoors. "My dad was a great family man and a very avid hunter and fisherman. Mom always talks about how dad would pack his hunting gear and the diaper bag and take me on hunting trips at a very early age," recalled Berringer.

On one hunting trip, Warren Berringer's truck broke down. "I guess he was working on the engine with a screwdriver and the screwdriver slipped and jabbed him in the eye. He ended up having an infection in the eye and following a cornea transplant, he contracted cancer. He lost his eye and after a five-year battle lost his bout with cancer, dying at age 39. I was in the second grade. The pain of losing my father became more intense as I grew older. I began really missing my dad and our family had to learn to rely on one another. The death ultimately made me stronger and after going through that tragedy, I felt prepared for any challenge."

Although his father is gone, the memories will never fade. "All of my memories of my dad involve the outdoors. I can remember in vivid detail a hunting trip I took with him when I was in kindergarten," said Berringer. "He taught me respect and love of the outdoors and I will have a great appreciation for that the rest of my life." Berringer holds the highest respect for his mother who was confronted with the challenge of raising three children alone. "She did an absolutely fabulous job taking care of us and instilling great values." Brook's older sister, Nicoel attends medical school, while his younger sister Drue is an undergraduate at Kansas State.

Not only does Brook have vivid and cherished memories of his father, he also has a special reminder of him through his Uncle William. "My dad and William were identical twins so I have obviously had a really special relationship with him. Through my uncle, I can see what my dad might have looked like and how he would have carried himself." William, who is now a pilot, played collegiate football with Brook's father at Colorado State. "William was the starting quarterback for four years and my dad walked-on and played half-back for one season and then decided to focus exclusively on his degree." It came as little surprise that Brook had some natural athletic ability and it didn't take him long to display that in his hometown, Goodland, Kansas.

Upon entering high school, Berringer made the transition from a starting receiver to the position he always longed to play — quarterback. "My freshman year in high school I saw some playing time and then was the starter for our junior varsity team as a sophomore," recalled Berringer. Going into his junior year, Berringer was torn between football and basketball. Berringer started some games for the varsity basketball team as a sophomore. "I really liked basketball more than football and thought I was better college material in basketball."

As luck would have it, Berringer's junior year of high school football was basically nonexistent as a result of a deep thigh bruise. The injury caused Berringer to see only limited action in the last few games of the season. "There I was at the end of my junior year and I had really had very little exposure as a football player. I thought I should get geared up for basketball." Berringer shifted his energies to the hard court and had an outstanding junior season and began drawing some attention from college basketball programs throughout the country. Still, few if any schools knew about Brook Berringer as a football player.

Before giving up on the idea of playing college football, Berringer hoped to turn some heads at prominent summer football camps. "The summer before my senior year, I decided to apply to attend Mile High Football Camp with the Denver Broncos and the Big Red Football School in Lincoln. I got accepted at the Mile High Camp but the Nebraska camp was already at capacity," recalled Berringer. Fortunately for Berringer, a friend in Goodland knew a former Husker strength and conditioning coach who was able to help get Brook accepted into Big Red Football School.

Berringer excelled at both the Mile High Camp and Big Red Football School. The highlight of the Mile High Camp was winning the eye-hand coordination drill with Gary Kubiak, who was the Broncos' backup quarter-back to John Elway. At the Nebraska camp, Berringer believes it was the combination of his passing skills and a big-time play he made in a touch football scrimmage that gained the attention of Husker head mentor, Tom Osborne. "I dropped back to pass and nobody was open so I scrambled and ran 50 yards for a touchdown. I remember Coach Osborne clapping and smiling along with making some notes in his notebook. At the con-clusion of the Nebraska camp, Coach Osborne con-firmed that he was impressed with me and told me his staff would be watching game film on me during my senior year and that if things went well they would like to offer me a scholarship."

Berringer was riding high upon returning to Good-land for his senior year and determined to close out his high school football career in grand style. He had a great senior year and as the season progressed, schools such as Kansas, Kansas State, Wyoming, Auburn and

Washington State emerged onto the recruiting scene. Flattered by the sudden interest, Berringer made an immediate verbal commitment to Coach Osborne and the Huskers.

"I really connected with Coach Osborne and Ron Brown. Plus, the outstanding facilities, academics, winning tradition and the fans gave Nebraska a total package that nobody else could compare to," recalled Berringer. "Nebraska was with me the whole way throughout the recruitment and kept in steady contact while other schools seemed to expect me to choose them and really didn't work at it quite as hard."

However, after just a couple days in Lincoln, Berringer was nearly ready to call it quits. "I wanted to come up earlier in the summer to go through the conditioning program and passing league to get a jump start. I just assumed that when I got here I would have a job and a place to stay, but quickly found out that wasn't the case," explained Berringer. "I called my mom and said 'I'm coming home' and she encouraged me to give everything a fair chance." Brook ended up sleeping on the floor in the apartment of former Husker fullback and Kansas native Lance Lewis.

For the moment, things appeared brighter. Berringer quickly discovered there weren't too many bright moments as a redshirt. "Once football started I felt things were even tougher...getting pounded on every day, knowing you're not going to play the whole season and basically feeling like a nobody. It was real tough." In the end, it was Berringer's perseverance that won out. "I have never been a quitter and I just told myself to take it one day at a time and that things would eventually get better. I really tried to improve every day as a scout team player and not just coast through the motions." Berringer survived 1991 and by 1992, as a redshirt freshman, he was convinced his situation would get better.

Berringer remembers when he first ran onto the turf at Memorial Stadium as a Husker. "At first I was really thinking about the game. I realized I was eligible to play, but probably was not going to play. Still, suited up as a Cornhusker, when I ran out onto the field I had an incredible rush of emotion. The sea of red, the fans, the noise all added up to an unbelievable experience. I never forgot that experience, and each time I took the field I had that same feeling of glory and excitement," said Berringer.

After his redshirt freshman season and seeing only limited duty in five games, Berringer was not satisfied with his progress. "At that time we had 12 or 13 quarterbacks and I just wasn't getting the repetitions I needed. It takes a while to grasp the offense and I knew I had to work on the little things to become a player. The coaches showed us what to do but they couldn't do it for us. If a player can't get the job done then someone else is always ready and capable."

Tommie Frazier proved to be the player who was capable of stepping in as a true freshman and winning the starting job over veteran Mike Grant. "I didn't get discouraged by Frazier's success; I knew I was a very capable athlete and all I needed was a chance to develop and show my skills," recalled Berringer. His opportunity to shine came early in 1993 during the first game of the season with North Texas State. Frazier sprained his ankle after only two series. "On my first drive I threw a touchdown pass to Corey Dixon and I will never forget that!" Berringer ended up with a great game and felt he had established himself as a capable starting quarterback. "Obviously North Texas wasn't a top-caliber team but I felt like that game earned me the trust and confidence of my teammates and coaches." Frazier returned the next week and wouldn't relinquish his starting role again until being sidelined by injury in the 1994 season.

At the end of the 1993 season, Berringer and the Huskers had earned a berth in the national championship game against Florida State in the 1994 Orange Bowl. Excited to be in a title game so early in his career, Berringer was far from being satisfied. "I wanted to be the guy out there doing it and not watching from the sidelines. I felt helpless and wanted in the worst way to become a more integral part of the team," concluded Berringer. Although he respected Frazier's ability, Berringer still strived for the starting position.

The Huskers came up short of winning the game, losing a heartbreaker to the Seminoles, 18-16. Despite the loss, Berringer and the Huskers were motivated to climb up the ranks. "We worked extremely hard through winter conditioning and the summer. The team made the decision early on to accept nothing less than a national title in 1994." The Frazier-led Huskers were well on their way to achieving that lofty goal when, in the fourth game of the season, Tommie Frazier was sidelined against Pacific with a sore calf and eventual blood clots. Again, Berringer was up to the task helping the Huskers on to victory.

It was early the next week, when Berringer was walking through South Stadium that someone stopped him and indicated that Frazier would be out for quite some time and might not play again in 1994. Though concerned over Frazier's injury, Berringer's perspective on his role in the remaining games changed immediately. "I remember getting an adrenalin rush and thinking that all of the sudden I'm the starter. It changed my whole outlook on the game and I had no doubts that I could handle the job," recalled Berringer.

While Berringer knew he could get the job, apparently the media questioned his ability. "All the questions dealt with my confidence level and inexperience. All that mattered to me was the faith the coaches and teammates had in me," said Berringer. He endeared himself to the Huskers and the nation in week five of the Huskers 1994 season playing against Wyoming. "I remember we were getting beat and with less than two minutes in the second quarter we went into the hurry-up offense. I completed seven passes and got the ball inside the 10-yard line with just a few seconds on the clock. On the next play, we ran a bootleg and scored but I took a hard hit resulting in five or six fractured ribs, with one of the ribs poking through and collapsing my lung," explained Berringer. In Berringer's eyes, it was that drive that proved to the nation he was a legitimate player and the team could still realize its national championship dream.

Despite the wicked hit to the ribs and a partially collapsed lung, Berringer hung tough and guided the Huskers to a victory in what proved to be one of the most difficult games of the 1994 campaign. After having his lung fully inflated and being fitted with a special protective flak jacket, Berringer was soon ready for his second game as a starter against Oklahoma State. "It was a conditional start. They told me that at halftime they would definitely take me to the University Health Center to take precautionary ex-rays just to make certain the lung was still fine." With about six minutes remaining in the first half, Berringer was running the option and knew immediately he had suffered a damaging blow. "The hit was very painful and I knew right away the lung had collapsed. It felt like the whole lung was piled up in the bottom of my stomach. I finished out the first half and then knew I was done." Berringer's lung was reinflated at halftime and he watched the remainder of the game from the sidelines. The "Turmanator" Matt Turman of Wahoo, Nebraska, quarterbacked the second half of the Oklahoma State game and through "quarterback by committee," the Huskers found themselves 6-0 and ready for a challenging midseason test on the road against Kansas State.

Leading up to the Kansas State game, discussion centered around the playing status of Brook Berringer. He made the trip to Manhattan and suited up; however, third string quarterback, Matt Turman, was given the start. Turman did an admirable job against a stingy Kansas State team. Coach Osborne decided to bring Berringer into the game late in the second quarter hoping to open up the offense. Berringer contributed to some big plays. Great running by Lawrence Phillips and Jeff Makovicka and a stifling defensive effort allowed the Huskers to survive with a 17-6 hard-fought win.

The following weekend Berringer sparkled at Missouri having an outstanding throwing day as he connected for three touchdowns en route to a 52-7 victory. It was the next game that Berringer was really looking toward to. "The homecoming game against Colorado was my chance to prove to the nation that Nebraska didn't take a step backward because of the loss of Tommie," said Berringer. Indeed, Berringer and the Huskers made a statement to the college football world playing a nearly flawless game, beating the Buffalos 24-7. "That game was our peak performance and we felt indestructible." Berringer and the Huskers were gradually earning national respect. The Huskers moved atop the college football rankings positioning themselves for another national championship game and Berringer silenced the media critics.

"I remember after the game doing a live interview on the set of ESPN's College Gameday. Corso and those guys were coming full circle saying that 'yes' Nebraska was a title contender with either me or Frazier at quarterback." While Berringer proved he could help lead the Huskers to the promised land in college football, Frazier had a challenging time with his new role as an inactive player. "Tommie is such a competitor that at times I felt like it was hard for him to be supportive of me," said Berringer.

In a year when the word "unity" took on new meaning in the Husker football program, the Huskers were slowly but surely becoming the nation's media darlings posting an 11-0 record, heading into the annual day-after-Thanksgiving rivalry with the Oklahoma Sooners. Frazier once again was in the headlines — this time not for his athleticism but simply for his availability. Frazier was cleared by doctors to take contact and was a late addition to the Nebraska travel roster departing for Norman. The availability of Frazier generated considerable distractions to the game, but according to Berringer, had no impact on his performance or the game. "My confidence level wasn't diminished by having Tommie in the wings. You can throw out the records when Nebraska and Oklahoma get together, especially knowing that OU had one of the best defenses in the nation. We knew we were in for a four quarter battle." Berringer and the Huskers persevered, taking over the Sooners in the fourth quarter, claiming a hard-fought 13-3 win, the Big Eight title and another shot at the national championship.

Even though he posted a 7-0 record as a Husker starter and earned second-team All-Big Eight honors, Berringer could not begin to rest on his laurels. Both Frazier and Berringer practiced well leading up to the 1995 Orange Bowl and national championship clash with Miami. It was at Orange Bowl media day that Coach Osborne announced that Frazier would get the start but both quarterbacks would see an equal amount of time. Berringer's reaction: "I was disappointed, but I had prepared myself for that decision. It was hard because we were both capable of getting the job done. I accepted the decision and still tried to be a good leader even though I wasn't starting." Still, Berringer knew he would see plenty of action. "The plan was for me to play the second quarter and then take things from there," recalled Berringer.

Berringer jump-started the Huskers, hitting tight end Mark Gilman on a 19-yard touchdown pass reducing the Hurricanes' lead to 10-7. "It was an overwhelming and fantastic feeling but it happened so quickly. With that play, I think our team and fans started to believe that we could win this game," explained Berringer.

Berringer started the third quarter and after a botched punt by Miami, Berringer and Nebraska were in scoring position once again when a Husker turnover occurred. "I was rolling out and simply trying to throw the ball away but didn't get it out of the end zone when a guy jumped up and picked it off. Had I thrown a touchdown pass on that play I feel I probably would have completed the game on the field and not the sidelines," said Berringer. Nebraska and Tom Osborne had a date with destiny in 1994 and that interception didn't figure into the outcome of the game.

Frazier sparkled in the fourth quarter and the blackshirts repeatedly put Frank Costa on his back. Two fourth-quarter touchdowns by Cory Schlesinger gave the Huskers an exhilarating 24-17 come-from-behind victory. Nebraska had its first football national championship since 1971. Berringer had mixed emotions about the game and the title. "The win was satisfying, yet I was disappointed I wasn't on the field at the end. It was tough watching the end of the game on the sidelines, but as always I tried to be supportive under the circumstances. I felt I contributed to the win and was a big part of the national championship."

Berringer said, "The neat thing about it was our team set specific goals and so many people stepped up when called upon to get the job done." He credits his friends and family for providing encouragement and support throughout a trying, yet rewarding season. "I learned a long time ago that the people you really play for are your family and friends. Those are the people I really celebrated with."

After the 1994 season, Berringer became a celebrity of sorts in Lincoln, especially with kids. "I spoke to countless schools and that was something I really enjoyed throughout my entire career. I've been fortunate to have positive role models in my life and I try to be the same for others," explained Berringer.

Berringer and Frazier headed into the 1995 fall camp as co-number one quarterbacks. A couple of days before the season opener at Oklahoma State, it was time for another decision. "Coach named Tommie the starter and again I had a feeling of disappointment but one I had tried to anticipate. I have always told myself that whether I started or not I was going to be a good leader both on and off the field."

When called upon, Berringer continued to prove that the Huskers had the best 1-2 quarterback combination in the country. Berringer played especially well in wins over Michigan State and Pacific before suffering traumatic bursitis in his right knee in the Washington State game. The injury sidelined Berringer for both the Missouri and Kansas State games; during Berringer's absence Frazier was in the midst of a Heisman Trophy-like season. "Tommie got on a roll and played very well. I was happy for Tommie but obviously didn't want my season to close out like it did. As the season wore on, I was watching lots of football from the sidelines and when you are a proven player, it hurts a little more," explained Berringer.

As a senior, Berringer was also concerned about the unjust scrutiny the Nebraska team and Coach Osborne endured. "None of us ever condoned what Lawrence Phillips did. Coach Osborne cares for all of us like we are his children and I will always have the utmost respect for him. He never shows favoritism and that results in high team unity. We all felt Lawrence received more than just punishment and that you don't desert your family and the people you care for," remarked Berringer. "Osborne always has to make tough decisions and unfortunately most of his concerning me went the other way. I'm not bitter to any degree, but I was hoping for a different ending to a very memorable career."

Most of Berringer's memorable Nebraska moments relate to the 1994 season. "My first start against Wyoming, beating Colorado in such a convincing fashion, starting against and beating arch-rival Oklahoma and figuring into the '95 championship game all stand out for me," recalled Berringer. Prior to playing in the 1996 Fiesta Bowl against Florida, Berringer added to his memories when walking across the stage at the Devaney Center to collect his degree in business administration. "It felt like a huge weight was lifted from my shoulders and was definitely one of my proudest moments in the past few years."

After graduation, there remained some business to take care of in Tempe, Arizona, against the Florida Gators. "Because of the way we dominated them, it seemed like just another win. The locker room wasn't very festive and I know the significance of going back-to-back won't be realized for many years to come when we are constantly referred to as a part of history — one of the greatest teams of all time," said Berringer. The 1995 Huskers were a special team and without question the 1995 seniors were a special group. "I think we are a very unique, close and special class that will maintain relationships well beyond Nebraska. I feel like I made friendships for a lifetime."

Brook Berringer hopes to take his football talents to the next level. "To make it in the NFL you have to be a great player and have some good fortune. I think I can play professionally but won't be devastated if I don't. I'm ready for the next chapter in my life and feel like I have several career options with business or aviation."

Brook Berringer has been a role model for the Nebraska football team and the entire university. "For me, my father was my role model because of his outstanding character. I owe so much to him and try to carry on his honor everyday. I think of him all of the time and I'm glad he was looking over me throughout a very memorable Nebraska career."

22
JEFF MAKOVICKA

Athletic bloodlines run in the Makovicka family. Jeff Makovicka's father, John, was a multi-sport star at the former Kearney State College, now University of Nebraska-Kearney. The elder Makovicka participated in multi-sports and earned All-American football honors. Makovicka's older sister, Jenny, played softball for a Kearney State team that went on to claim a national championship and younger brother Joel currently plays fullback for the Nebraska Cornhuskers.

Although he came from a sports-oriented family, Jeff was never pushed into athletics. "My father left the decision up to me and made it clear he would support me with or without sports," recalled Makovicka. "It was my choice to pursue athletics and I felt fortunate to have a father who could guide me throughout the whole process. I really didn't get serious about sports until the seventh grade. When I first stepped onto a football field I had so much excitement and energy built up in me that I was ready to go after it." Not only did Makovicka possess the energy and intensity that often takes athletes to the next level, he inherited a special intangible characteristic. "I hated getting beat and have always been a super-competitive person."

Makovicka also has had to display patience during his athletic career. Continuing to play ball in high school, Makovicka had to work hard to make the starting team. In fact, despite rushing for over 4,000 career yards at East Butler High School in Brainard, Nebraska, Makovicka didn't start until his junior season. "When people find out that I didn't start at a small school until my junior year, they assume I wasn't a very good player," said Makovicka. The fact that Makovicka played eight-man football caused people to wonder if he would play in the college ranks. "I used all of the speculation to my advantage. The bottom line is I have two arms, two legs and a head on my shoulders and I'm just as capable as the next guy. People think if you played eight-man ball or come from a small town, you are an alien on the football field," remarked Makovicka.

Makovicka ended up leading East Butler High School to a D-1 State Championship as a junior and was a two-year All-State player. Despite having impressive credentials, college football recruiters were not blazing a trail to the Makovicka household. "I always wanted to go to Nebraska and actually inquired about walking-on and at first they told me I wasn't fast enough or big enough. That made me mad and I thought to myself that I would go to Oklahoma and come back someday and make a statement by beating the Huskers." Makovicka continued to send his highlight tapes around and received interest from various schools including Iowa State, Colorado State, Kansas State, Oklahoma and

Oklahoma State. "Everyone with the exception of Nebraska and Oklahoma was thrilled about the prospects of me walking-on. Before I selected another school, I wanted to make one last effort to Nebraska. I wanted every coach to see my tapes and was optimistic about becoming a Husker," recalled Makovicka.

By May, at high school graduation, classmates were asking each other about future plans. "Everyone was wondering where I was going to college and who I was going to play for. I told them I had no idea. About one week later, my father got a call from Coach Osborne at work who said 'We would like your son to walk-on at Nebraska.'" Makovicka was excited. "I was really happy, especially since it was one of the first years where they really limited the number of walk-ons invited to come in." Thrilled that he was headed to Nebraska, Makovicka was even more honored to be playing for Coach Tom Osborne. "Many people feel he is one of the most important people in the state and then I had the chance to meet him in person. At first I was kind of in awe of him. He is a very soft spoken and positive person who truly cares about student-athletes."

The beginning of two-a-days during his freshman year in 1991 was a real eye opener for Makovicka. "The first time I met my teammates and the coaches was during fall camp. I didn't know anyone. I checked into a dorm room with two bags over my shoulders and saw a 300-pound lineman, Christian Peter, and immediately asked myself, 'What in the heck am I doing here?'" But Makovicka was convinced if he could just make it through the first couple of weeks, he could adjust to the Big Red program.

In the beginning, Makovicka's master plan at Nebraska was to play scout team, make the team, possibly contribute, get a letter jacket and hopefully walk away with at least one Big Eight championship ring. "Once I started hitting some guys in practice, it all changed. I remember after the first practice calling my father and telling him 'I think I can play here.'" After redshirting his first year at Nebraska in 1991, good times were just around the corner for the versatile Makovicka who played both I-back and fullback.

Makovicka beat the odds and made the travel roster as a redshirt freshman. "That was a great accomplishment for me and I think it showed the coaches what kind of work ethic and determination I had." Makovicka saw action in seven games as a reserve I-back but was far from discouraged. "I knew it would be a gradual progression for me to become a starter. I was willing to pay my dues but really wanted to contribute anyway that I could," explained Makovicka. Even though making the travel roster was the highlight of Makovicka's redshirt freshman season, he will never forget the feeling of entering Memorial Stadium on game day as a player for the first time.

"I think I had a sore neck after that day from straining to see everything — the crowd, the red, the balloons. It was all totally unbelievable." Early on in his career, Makovicka had to concentrate on staying focused while on the field with the awesome fan support at Memorial Stadium. "I remember being in my stance on the field and looking into the stands and not being able to concentrate on the call or the snap count. It takes time to learn to deal with the crowd and also become zoned-in on football and your opponent." Makovicka also recalls getting called into the game during his first season when the Huskers played at Oklahoma. "I remember having the game taped and hearing ABC announcer Keith Jackson call my name. I thought that was so neat that he pronounced my name on national television because I grew up listening to that guy. My freshman year, those little things meant so much."

In the 1993 season, Makovicka's redshirt sophomore year, he played in all eleven games and scored three touchdowns on the road to the Huskers' national championship showdown with Florida State in the 1994 Orange Bowl game.

Toward the end of the '93 campaign, Makovicka made a position move to fullback and was second on the depth chart behind Cory Schlesinger. "The coaches had a feeling that a quick trap might work well against Florida State. I remember on the day of the game, Coach Osborne asked me if I was ready. He said 'I think that trap play will work and I want you to be ready and stay by Coach Gill on the sidelines,'" recalled Makovicka. Eager for the challenge and the opportunity, Makovicka was anxious, considering he was relatively new at the fullback position. "The first play I was in the game, Frazier audibled to a 32 option and it was a busted play. Even though we didn't execute the play, that was a key moment in my career because of the faith the coaches showed in me."

The breaks did not go Nebraska's way at the Orange Bowl as Florida State prevailed in a dramatic 18-16 victory. Makovicka recalls, "It was almost better than a win because coming so close left that bad taste in our mouths. Coach Osborne told us we did win that night and the nation did know that we were the best team in the country. That statement set the tone for spring ball and summer conditioning. I never saw so much drive and determination to get back to the big dance as I did that season."

In the spring of 1994, Makovicka was summoned to Coach Osborne's office. "I wondered why he wanted to talk to me. I was thrilled when he explained there was a scholarship for me due to the mid-term graduation of a senior. For me, a walk-on, that was the biggest day of my life. I really felt valued, like I was permanently a part of the program," recalled Makovicka.

Preparing for his junior campaign and still raw at the fullback position, Makovicka came to rely heavily on the advice of starting fullback Cory Schlesinger. "Cory wasn't threatened by me as his backup and did everything in his power to help me. We were roommates on road games and really became close friends who supported one another," recalled Makovicka. Makovicka was quick to return the favor to Schlesinger. "Coach Solich was up in the press box during the games, so I could share with Cory a different perspective from the sideline. He would come off the field and I could tell him about a better angle he could take on a linebacker or just anything to give him an edge."

Perhaps the biggest lesson Makovicka learned from Schlesinger was how to practice. "Cory was the best practice player we've ever had. He went full-speed on every play and that is something that I tried to carry over into my senior season." The fullback duo of Schlesinger and Makovicka proved to be dynamic, totaling 777 yards on 110 carries. With quarterback injuries to both Tommie Frazier and Brook Berringer, other positions had to step up and they did. Never was that more true than in the 1994 Nebraska at Kansas State game.

"For me the Kansas State game was one of my career highlights because I established myself as a go-to guy. Things weren't clicking as usual for Cory and he had a fumble so the coaches decided to go with me in the fourth quarter. I wanted to do well so badly, since I was in the game when the outcome was still on the line." Makovicka responded in a big way, rushing for 56 fourth-quarter yards and a game-clinching touchdown. "I was glad they didn't have the celebration rule that year because I was so fired up after that touchdown. I was jumping all over the place and I will never forget that Schlesinger was one of the first guys to congratulate me as I was running off the field," said Makovicka.

To Makovicka, the Kansas State game also symbolized the 1994 team. "All we wanted was to win. It didn't matter who was in at what position. Whatever it took to get the job done and become national champions was our only focus." Makovicka and the Huskers had a date with destiny on January 1, 1995, in the Orange Bowl against Miami.

"I remember the night before the game in the hotel room telling Cory that I thought he was going to have a big game and he was like, 'Yeah... whatever.' The coaching staff and all of the players were very confident going into the game and we felt that eventually the game would be ours." And...just as Makovicka had predicted, Schlesinger was outstanding. Schlesinger scored on two fourth-quarter trap plays giving the Huskers a come-from-behind, dramatic 24-17 win over the Miami Hurricanes. "I was so happy for Cory and for the whole team. It was a total team effort as both the offense and defense gave it their all," remarked a smiling Makovicka. "Our lives changed because we now ended the season as winners. I had hated coming back to campus as a loser after a bowl game. It was like all the other wins were meaningless and that we were only a good team in the conference and not the elite team in the country," said Makovicka.

Another special twist to the 1994 National Championship was the fact that Makovicka's younger brother Joel was able to be a part of it. "I remember after Joel committed to Nebraska, we did an interview and talked about how neat it would be to have two national championship rings in the family. For that to come true right away was amazing," said Makovicka. Joel Makovicka redshirted in 1994 and played backup fullback in 1995.

The 1995 season proved to be a challenging one for Jeff Makovicka and the Huskers. Makovicka earned the starting fullback spot and was part of one of the most explosive backfields in the country with the likes of Heisman candidates Tommie Frazier at quarterback and Lawrence Phillips at I-back. Makovicka and Phillips operated as one on the field and through football became friends. "After the big games Lawrence put up against Oklahoma State and Michigan State, I felt I was blocking for the next Heisman Trophy winner. When I heard the news about Lawrence's assault charge against his former girlfriend, I was devastated. It was tough losing a teammate and I just began hoping that he would get the help he needed to turn his life around. The neat thing about sports is it brings people together from different walks of life. You become brothers with your teammates regardless of their backgrounds and that is really a positive experience. Nebraska football becomes your family for five years and it's hard to not become attached to your teammates and coaches."

"I remember right before the '95 Orange Bowl against Miami, Coach Osborne seemed as though he really needed the win to silence the critics and help him catch his second wind in coaching. After the win, Coach Osborne seemed to have a new hop in his step and he really seemed to be thriving in his position. Then after the incident with Lawrence Phillips and some of the other things that came up, I felt as if we were in jeopardy of losing the best football coach in the country," recalled Makovicka. "He went from bringing home the 1994 National Championship and being referred to as a great coach to a guy the media was determined to tear down. My heart truly went out to the man and our team became committed to easing his pain through our actions on the field," remarked Makovicka.

Makovicka and the Huskers finished the regular season 11-0 in 1995 and earned a berth in their third consecutive national championship game, this time against the Florida Gators in the 1996 Fiesta Bowl. The Huskers were not to be denied. They dominated the Gators, scoring a 62-24 win. "I could have never imagined closing out my career with a game like that. That night, Nebraska earned a place in football history and I just feel very proud and fortunate to be a part of it all."

Jeff Makovicka has definitely etched his name in Husker history. His photo appeared in *Sports Illustrated* magazines. His football future remains up in the air. "I'm not sure if I've played my last football game. I feel I have the best football years ahead of me and that I can definitely make a National Football League team. I hope I get a chance because I believe I can open some eyes and open up my game." Every good football player knows the meaning of option and Makovicka has a backup plan in the event pro football doesn't materialize.

"My dad is a physical therapist and I've really seen the impact that helping others can have. He helped a young lady who was in a wheelchair to walk again and that was so rewarding for him. I want to be involved with rehabilitation and really make a difference in the lives of others," said Makovicka.

The Makovicka legacy at Nebraska will continue for three more years as Jeff's younger brother Joel prepares to compete for the starting fullback position. "He is going to be a lot better than I ever was because he got a jump-start on big-time football. When he was in high school I was always telling him the little extra things he should do to become a great player. He has done that and then some. I know he has a very bright future," explained Makovicka.

Jeff Makovicka has an equally promising future. He has the heart and desire and that's going to take him a long way in this world. Just like the entire Makovicka family, he has something people can't measure.

26

CLINTON CHILDS

Gifted runner and versatile athlete Clinton Childs always had a burning desire to compete against the best. Childs was introduced to athletics at the tender age of four.

"Wrestling was the first sport I got involved with and I liked it from the very beginning. My cousins, Phillip Doolittle and Duane Childs, taught me the finer aspects of the sport and were positive influences in my life. I really liked the fact that wrestling was one-on-one. I was solely responsible for the outcome. In the end, the best man wins," remarked Childs. In high school, Childs was the best man in wrestling. He closed out his Omaha North High School wrestling career by claiming the gold medal in the Class A 189-pound division during his senior year. "It was a really good feeling and something I'm still very proud of."

Childs also had a stellar high school football career. During his junior year, Childs was among the best Nebraska high school running backs. He racked up 1,428 yards. As a senior, Childs put up even bigger numbers, totaling 1,495 yards. Childs garnered first-team All-State honors and was named a Blue Chip All-American.

Childs received national recruiting attention from schools seeking both his football and wrestling skills. "I thought football would present the best options down the road," said Childs of his decision to pursue football in college. Childs saw pros and cons about staying in state and becoming a Husker. "Growing up in Omaha, Nebraska, I went through a time when I was certain I wanted to go out of state. On the other hand, I thought staying in state would allow me to have the support of my family and friends," recalled Childs.

Childs, who played both running back and inside linebacker in high school, was recruited by many big-time college programs and eventually narrowed his choices to Kansas and Nebraska. "I remember how successful Gale Sayers was at Kansas and I felt that maybe I could be the next Omaha player to become a star at Kansas. I also liked the fact it would be fairly close to home." Eventually, it was Nebraska's tradition that won Childs over. "I am the type of person who hates to lose. Nebraska was winning and was ranked at the top of the polls. That was a big factor in my decision," remarked Childs.

"I also knew that the best I-backs always went to Nebraska and I was excited to see how I would stack up against the nation's elite. I felt I could hold my own because some of the best backs in the nation came right out of Omaha." Childs had to wait an extra year to see what impact he would have in the Nebraska backfield.

"Sitting out in 1992 for academic reasons was tough but maybe a blessing in disguise. I tried to turn the situation into a positive and get focused as a student. After I made it through that year, I felt I could overcome anything," explained Childs.

Starting behind the eight ball as a first-year player in 1993, Childs knew it would be a challenging first year on the field. "I was realistic and knew it would be a tough adjustment. Still, I was just hoping to get a chance to showcase my talents." Childs experienced Nebraska's rich I-back tradition first-hand, playing backup to starter Calvin Jones along with freshmen Damon Benning and Lawrence Phillips and sophomore Jeff Makovicka. Childs saw limited action in five games and scored his first Husker career touchdown against Iowa State. A sprained ankle kept Childs out of action in the 1994 Orange Bowl against Florida State. "I wanted so badly for the players and Coach Osborne to be on the winning team at the end of that game. Even though we lost, I think there was some comfort knowing everyone gave it their very best shot," concluded Childs.

Childs was ready to give the game his best shot as a junior in 1994. He was in continuous competition with Omaha friend Damon Benning to emerge as the backup I-back to Lawrence Phillips. "I am a very intense player and enjoyed competing with guys like Damon and Lawrence. All of the backs supported one another, and even though we were competitive we never got jealous. Jealousy would have been disruptive to our team goals," remarked Childs.

Childs accepted his role in the Husker backfield, but it wasn't always easy. "It was tough not being the go-to guy. I really felt like I had the ability to be a starter anywhere in the country. I felt like there wasn't much drop-off between any of the I-backs and that all of us could have done the job when called upon," said Childs. When his number was called, Childs responded. He ran for nearly 400 yards and was a valuable kickoff return man during his junior campaign.

Before the chapter closed on Childs' junior season, the Huskers won the 1995 Orange Bowl. "I was so happy Nebraska finally won a national title and that I was able to contribute to the championship. We felt like Coach Osborne deserved one many years ago and we were glad to be the team to share it with him. The feeling of satisfaction felt so good that everyone continued working hard throughout the summer and we were ready to go after the repeat," described Childs.

Childs, who had dreamed of playing Sunday football in the National Football League since age nine, was optimistic about going out in style during his senior year. Childs got his chance in 1995, due, in large part, to the suspension of starter Lawrence Phillips. "I was sad for Lawrence. As a friend, I told him he had my support and that no matter what happened he should keep his head up," remarked Childs.

"I always found Lawrence to be a very outgoing and friendly person. We never talked football off the field; he just wanted to be a normal guy. We enjoyed going out to the mall and just getting away." Clinton and Lawrence often got away to Omaha to spend time at the Childs' household. "My family opened their arms to Lawrence. My mother really established a good friendship with him."

Shortly after the Phillips suspension, Childs was slated for his first career start against Arizona State, Nebraska's third game of the 1995 season. "I was more than ready for the start. I saw this as a chance to prove to everyone, including myself that I'm no ordinary backup," said Childs.

It didn't take long for Childs to prove that Husker I-backs were some of the very best in the country. On Nebraska's first play from scrimmage, Childs sprinted 65 yards to the end zone, making a statement to the Sun Devils and to the nation. Childs ended the day with a career-high 143 yards on 12 carries and scored two touchdowns in Nebraska's 77-28 victory. Childs was forced to make an early exit as a result of a strained knee. The injury ultimately sidelined him for the next two games.

Childs was forced to the role of "cheerleader" for a couple of weeks and watched Damon Benning and Ahman Green fill in admirably during his absence. He would not regain his position as a starter. "Damon did a good job and Ahman proved he was worthy of all the pre-season hype. I was supportive of Ahman at all times and after I got healthy was determined to make the most of my carries whenever called upon," said Childs.

"By 1995, our confidence and unity was so strong, we expected to win the second championship. I gave the offensive line lots of credit and feel like they were one of the major parts to our 'taking care of business,'" remarked Childs. It was business as usual for the Huskers — they dominated the Gators from start to finish in the 1996 Fiesta Bowl.

"Tom Osborne and the Nebraska program has changed me from a kid to a man. Even though my football career didn't exactly pan out the way I had hoped, I learned so many important lessons of life," said Childs. "Coach Tom Osborne taught me about loyalty and honesty. He is a very honest man who stuck behind me and all of the players one hundred percent at all times." Childs credited his mother, Linda, and late grandmother, Mary Carter, as his primary role models. "They have always been there for me and supported me in everything I did. They always stressed how important it was for me to stay involved with sports. My older brothers Ken and Cal have also been positive figures in my life."

Childs also believes that athletics helped him avoid some of the pitfalls often associated with North Omaha, the inner city where he grew up. "When I talk with kids and youth groups back home, I tell them to get involved in something that will focus them in a positive direction. Everyone has special talents, it's just a matter of figuring out what they are," said Childs.

Should pro football not be in Childs' future, North Omaha might be. "I would like to do some counseling in North Omaha to educate kids about gangs and other negatives. If it weren't for the Omaha Bears Wrestling Program and the Boy's Club, I wouldn't be where I am today."

27

JACQUES ALLEN

Some athletes take offense at being labeled as a "role player." Jacques Allen, a product of Kansas City, Missouri, took great pride in playing several key roles for the Nebraska Cornhusker football team.

Early indicators predicted Allen had the ability to be an impact player in almost any sport. "My father got me started at around age eight playing football, basketball and baseball. Early on, I really loved baseball and thought it would be my sport of preference in the long run." Allen credits the determination of his father, Jerry Allen, for giving him the opportunity to attend Raytown High School in Kansas City. "I was raised on 74th Street in Kansas City and that was considered a pretty rough neighborhood. My parents were teachers as I was growing up and my Dad pursued additional education with the goal of getting an even better job," explained Allen.

Jerry Allen succeeded in his mission to place his family in a better environment with fewer distractions. "At first I was very upset and didn't want to move away from my friends. I had my moments when I got into trouble, so I guess it was good we moved," said Allen. The Allen family relocated to south Kansas City, where

Mr. Allen became the principal at Grandview High School. Jacques' mother, Gloria, is a ninth grade English teacher. "My parents did everything to keep me away from trouble and put me in an environment where I could be successful."

Allen became quite successful at Raytown High School where he earned second-team All-State honors as a senior receiver and free safety. During his high school career, Allen caught 73 passes for 1,350 yards and made a school record 27 touchdowns. With impressive statistics and a ton of confidence, Allen was ready to take his show to the next level. "I looked at Nebraska, Kansas State, Kansas, Missouri and a few other major programs. I was offered some scholarships at smaller schools but was really looking for the place that could provide a total program. It was obvious Nebraska was concerned about me as a complete person, student and player. Those factors outweighed a scholarship," said Allen.

Arriving at Nebraska in 1991, Allen was determined to catch the coaching staff's attention and prove he was a quality athlete. "I didn't want to be considered a guy who just hung on to the team and didn't make a contribution." After redshirting in 1991, Allen learned to make meaningful contributions off the playing field; he didn't see action in 1992 as a redshirted freshman wingback.

Allen was quickly becoming a role player for the Huskers — his role: keeping the atmosphere loose and stress-free for his Husker teammates and coaches. "Everyone called me the joker or comedian. If my actions helped put people in a more relaxed mood, then I felt like I did something positive. I could tell by facial expressions that I had a positive impact on many people." Allen was widely known for his countless character impersonations. Perhaps his most famous was that of Fire Marshal Bill from the TV comedy *In Living Color.*

Allen was one of the few Nebraska players who could send Coach Tom Osborne into a laughing frenzy. "It was a challenge to get him to crack-up but he was always a good sport about all of my kidding around. I really think deep down he appreciated the mood I tried to create and I know the guys loved seeing me joke with him," remembered Allen.

Even though he saw limited playing time throughout his Nebraska career, Allen never considered football a joke. "I was all business on the practice field. I always wanted to have exceptional practices and go all out on every play. I think some of the guys thought it was crazy to go that hard as a scout team member, but I felt it was best for the team. I knew our defense would be going against some of the best in the country and I tried to give them a similar picture in practice. I pretended every practice was a national championship game, and I went full-tilt every play. Heck, I would even talk some noise to the guys."

In the long run, Allen is convinced he earned the respect of his teammates and coaches for his actions on the practice field. "The top guys would say I really helped get them prepared, that they appreciated my effort. That made me feel satisfied!" said Allen.

Allen apparently did a great job in helping prepare the top units for some of the nation's finest. Even though he didn't get on the field during the 1995 Orange Bowl, the thrill of victory was intense for Allen. "I put in just as many hours at practice as the starters did. I felt I played an important role in that first national title," said Allen. "I think I experienced every emotion possible and once we got that first one I knew we had the confidence for a second title."

After playing four games in his junior season, Allen saw action in a total of seven games as a Husker senior. "I was pleased with the way I progressed and, of course, closing out my career with another championship was simply amazing," said Allen.

Another amazing experience at Nebraska was the chance to play for and get to know Dr. Tom Osborne. "Coach Osborne is a good all-around man. He has been nothing but true to me and all of the players. Coach always makes you feel wanted and important. He has an open door policy to all current and former players. What a tremendous honor to be a part of his great program," summarized Allen.

Coach Tom Osborne produces All-Americans on the football field and Academic All-Americans in the classroom. Osborne also develops adolescents into young men. "I've matured a great deal at Nebraska and realize the importance of trying to make good decisions," remarked Allen. In fact, Allen often encouraged youngsters to make good decisions in life and to stay in school through motivational rap music.

Nebraska football has inspired Allen to help youngsters with motivational rap music. "I've always had the ability to come up with verses that have a good message for kids. I try to remember my childhood and the lessons my parents taught me. All of that combined makes for some cool rap songs that the kids can really relate to," explained Allen. Allen would often rap with former Husker split-end Corey Dixon at the annual "School is Cool" Jam in front of thousands of youth from all over the state of Nebraska. "I enjoyed performing for the kids and the messages I gave have made me more accountable as a student and person."

After earning his college diploma, Allen plans to return to Kansas City to once again become a valuable "role player." "I would like to work for a community or recreational center for youth. They need programs like that to help kids," remarked Allen. According to Jacques, he and his younger brother, Victor, have beat the odds of inner-city ills. "We owe it all to our parents. They are role models to us and to the kids they teach every day at school," said Allen.

When reflecting on his Nebraska career, Jacques points to senior day against the Oklahoma Sooners as a day that stands out in his mind. "As I ran out on the field by myself, the whole crowd was applauding even though most didn't know who I was. To me they were saying 'thank you for sticking it out and being there every day. You were a big part of the program!'"

Jacques Allen has left his mark on the Nebraska football program. Allen will be remembered as the team comedian who was the ultimate scout team player. Allen is a young man committed to giving back to youth so that they can also become premiere "role players" in the game of life.

33

CLESTER JOHNSON

Sylvo Johnson, Clester's brother and legal guardian wasn't a huge Cornhusker fan in the early 1990s. "He said Nebraska couldn't win the big one and lost bowl games all the time," recalled Clester Johnson. Little did Sylvo know that his younger brother would eventually play a key role in altering such attitudes.

Johnson moved to Bellevue, Nebraska, to join his brother Sylvo after being raised by his aunt and uncle due to the untimely death of his mother. Johnson was a multi-talented athlete at Bellevue West High School. There he earned All-State quarterback honors, gold medals in the 110-meter high and 300-meter hurdles, and Class A runner-up honors in the 189-pound wrestling class as a senior. Not surprisingly, Johnson drew national interest from many colleges in football, track and wrestling. "Most of the Big Eight schools recruited me in addition to schools like Ol' Miss, Iowa, Indiana and Illinois," remembered Johnson.

"I was about ready to become an Iowa Hawkeye when the Nebraska coaches told me how important it was to keep the in-state guys at home. I also felt that if I had a decent career, the recognition I might gain as a Husker football player could help me after college." With impressive high school credentials and plenty of confidence, Johnson was convinced he would make an immediate impact for the Big Red.

"I received a rude awakening when I got a taste of the competition during my first exposure to Nebraska football. It was an adjustment going from a prime time player to a practice player." Johnson let it be known from the beginning that he felt the starting job was his for the taking, but some of the veterans took exception to his zeal. "Guys like Mike Grant would tease me since I thought I could come in and start right away. Some of the other guys labeled me as a guy with an attitude," recalls Johnson.

Johnson agrees that his attitude was not the best in 1991 during his redshirt freshman year. "It seemed like that year we were flooded with quarterback prospects and I felt like I wasn't getting enough repetitions to establish myself as a player. One day after working out in the weight room I think Coach Osborne could sense I was down and disappointed. We talked about trying a different position and he told me I was a good enough athlete that he thought I could fill a need in the secondary." During spring ball, the versatile Johnson made the jump from quarterback to cornerback. Said Johnson, "All I remember was getting humiliated in the Spring Game by Duane Wiles. I was beginning to think that Nebraska just wasn't the place for me and maybe I needed to look into other options." Fortunately for Nebraska and Johnson, he decided to confer with secondary coach, George Darlington. Darlington referred

Johnson to receivers' coach Ron Brown who immediately liked what he saw. "He compared me to Nate Turner because of my size and physical style and thought I could become a really good wingback." It was like starting all over for Johnson, in essence, a second consecutive redshirt year.

In 1992 as a redshirt freshman, Johnson played in four regular season games as a reserve wingback before making his move during his second round with spring football. "I took it upon myself to become a student of the game and stop hanging out with the wrong crowd," recalled Johnson, known by his teammates as "CJ." Johnson's new attitude began paying immediate dividends as he climbed to fourth on the wingback depth chart. "My goal was to become a solid third on the depth chart during fall camp; I knew that would allow me to see playing time and probably make the travel roster." Johnson realized his goal, becoming the number three wingback in 1993 and earning a spot on the travel squad. And his steady climb wasn't over. After an impressive game against North Texas State, he solidified himself as the backup to Abdul Muhammad and played in all eleven regular season games as well as in the 1994 Orange Bowl against Florida State.

Johnson credits the improvement in football as the key to his turnaround in the classroom. "Some guys think if you are a star on the field you are destined for the pros and can forget the books. I saw that I had the ability to reach my goal as a football player and then became convinced I could do the same in the classroom." Despite losing the Orange Bowl and the national championship in heartbreaking fashion, CJ and his returning teammates were determined to get the job done in 1994.

"I thought I had a legitimate chance of being a starter during my junior year in '94 and felt I could become a go-to-receiver in the clutch," explained Johnson. Johnson and his fellow receivers were often acknowledged more for their blocking prowess than catching ability. "Receivers at Nebraska have to accept that there just aren't going to be that many big pass plays and you must become a good downfield blocker in order to see the field." At 210 pounds, Johnson established himself as a punishing blocker and very reliable receiver. According to plan, CJ opened the 1994 season as the starting wingback against West Virginia in the Kickoff Classic.

Thrilled with the opportunity to start, Johnson had the chance to put up a quick six points early in the game, but it was not to be. "I missed a ball that should have been for a touchdown and the pass was intercepted by a West Virginia defensive back. I guess that play messed with my confidence somewhat and I think the coaching staff lost some of their confidence in me," remembered Johnson. With the exception of a start against UCLA, Johnson was relegated to the role of Abdul Muhammad's backup. Johnson played in all of the Huskers' thirteen victories on the road to the Huskers' first football national crown since 1971. "It felt good to beat Miami and become national champions but still, I wasn't the player I knew I could be," said Johnson.

The goal-oriented Johnson had his coming-out party in the 1995 season and, just as he hoped, became the team's clutch receiver and starting wingback. "My senior season was a very satisfying year because I felt like the coaches had faith in my ability and my teammates started to recognize me as a key contributor to the team."

Johnson more than filled the void left by former player Abdul Muhammad, becoming the Huskers' leading receiver with 22 grabs for 367 yards on the season and two scores. Johnson's most memorable game came against Arizona State in his senior year — he snagged four balls for a career-best 129 yards, hitting pay dirt once. Said Johnson, "I felt I could do no wrong that game and had a great sense of satisfaction considering all of the position changes and patience I went through to get to that point."

There were many more special feelings in store for Johnson during 1995. The last time he entered Memorial Stadium prior to the annual Oklahoma showdown produced a blur of flashbacks. "I really felt good about the way my career was closing out and that all of the tough times were definitely for a reason. I hugged Coach Osborne and was glad my family was in attendance, but I really didn't get sad like I expected," remembered Johnson.

After the Huskers beat the Sooners, the good times kept rolling for Johnson. In mid-December, he suited up again, this time in the Devaney Sports Center wearing a cap and gown for commencement exercises. Johnson collected his college diploma, earning a degree in sociology in four and one-half years. "Most people said I wouldn't graduate from college so it was a pretty amazing feeling. I remember sitting at graduation and daydreaming, not believing that I was in the company of all the other graduates. Graduation was a great accomplishment for me and I know I shocked a lot of people back home."

Johnson's college diploma was without question one of his biggest catches during his NU career. Even though he had already secured five Big Eight championship rings and one national championship diamond, he was determined to go out on top. "Everyone says the 1994 title was for Coach Osborne. Maybe it was, but I really felt like the team gave it their all in 1995 mainly because of the doubters all across the nation," said Johnson. "Tom Osborne is a living legend who always talks to the players about being a good citizen, raising a family and having a spiritual life to get through the tough times. The team was bothered by the heat Coach Osborne was taking for the players and we decided to use the off-the-field problems to our advantage," explained Johnson.

Johnson and the Huskers put it all together during the 1996 Fiesta Bowl, ringing up a 62-24 victory against the highly touted Florida Gators. "The second championship showed the domination and character of the Nebraska football team. Our guys seem to have a history of overcoming the odds with Tommie Frazier's injury in 1994 and the adversity we experienced in 1995," reflected Johnson.

When the game clock ticked down to zero at Sun Devil Stadium, it brought an end to Johnson's Husker playing days. "I tried to stay on the field as long as I possibly could, savoring every last moment as a Husker. I sought out interviews so I would have the chance to express to all of the Nebraska fans just how much they meant to our team's success."

Johnson's Nebraska football career encompassed numerous position changes and he developed invaluable personal traits on the long journey to becoming an NU starter and impact player. His rewards were many, ranging from friendships to seven championship rings and a treasured college degree. Clester Johnson is ready to write the next chapter of his life. The content will include his quest to take his game to the next level. One thing is for certain, Clester Johnson will be a winner in the game of life, much like he was a winner in his Nebraska career.

37

DARReN SCHMADEKe

Husker cornerback Darren Schmadeke accomplished what many Husker faithful only dream about. The 5-8, 175-pound player lived out a fantasy coming to the University of Nebraska and leaving as a champion. Schmadeke's dream began taking shape in Albion, Nebraska. "Our family lived two miles outside of Albion on an acreage. Our home was up on a hill so my brother and I were constantly outside running up and down the hill," recalled Schmadeke.

The running apparently paid off for Darren and twin brother Damon who both excelled in track at an early age. "By age ten, we could tell that we had some ability. We both ran in The Athletic Congress (TAC) and had some success," said Schmadeke. The Schmadeke twins and parents Ralph and Debbie spent many summers traveling around the country in a motor home to national track meets. The twins competed in three national meets with Darren's best performance being a 5th place finish in the 100 meters. "It was a rewarding experience and a good opportunity for our family to spend time together."

Darren and Damon, not surprisingly, went on to spend lots of time together in athletics. "We went to many football camps together. We went down to the Big Red Football School for four years. I think that helped us get some exposure with the Nebraska coaches. It was exciting being coached by some of the greatest in the game." The Schmadeke brothers also attended the Lou Holtz football camp in South Bend, Indiana. "The biggest difference between camps was that the Notre Dame camp had several guest coaches and only a few of the Notre Dame staff were involved," said Schmadeke.

Darren totaled 1,900 career rushing yards at Albion High School where he played running back, free safety, linebacker and punter. An All-Conference and All-State selection, Schmadeke set the school record in the 100-meter dash at 10.44 and won state in the C-1 100 and 200 meters.

Shortly after his senior season, Schmadeke began receiving calls and letters about his football future. "I received scholarship offers to Wayne State College and Doane in Nebraska, and considered walking-on at the University of South Dakota, Kansas State, Colorado and of course, Nebraska. It had always been a dream of mine to come to Nebraska and play for the Huskers."

Important to Schmadeke was a good academic program and the chance to expand horizons. "I grew up in a small town and pretty much ruled out going to college in a small town." Schmadeke and his family made three campus visits. One of the gauges he used to rate the schools' programs: the meals. "At Nebraska

they served a really classy prime rib lunch. At Kansas
State it was pizza and pop. South Dakota provided
Oreo cookies and said lunch was on our own."
Schmadeke was impressed by all aspects of the Ne-
braska program and was optimistic he would get the
opportunity to walk on at Nebraska.

"I'll never forget the night quarterback coach
Turner Gill called our home and invited my brother
and me to walk on to the Nebraska program," said
Darren. We grew up watching the Huskers and players
like Turner Gill and now we both had a chance to be
a part of Nebraska football."

The adjustment from stardom at Albion High
School to Nebraska football as a freshman in 1991 was
something Schmadeke was prepared for. "I knew I was
going to be at the ground level. I was just glad to be a
part of the team and was willing to pay my dues on
the scout team." Schmadeke also played on the junior
varsity team in 1991, the last year the Huskers were
allowed to field such a team. The scout team experience was a trying one for Schmadeke. "It seemed nobody cared much about you and it was very physically
demanding. It was something you just had to take and
try to get through." There were moments when
Schmadeke had his doubts. "It did cross my mind to
give it all up and just be a college student. I know
many people doubted if a small-town kid could make
it, and I used that everyday to keep hanging in there,"
said Schmadeke.

Schmadeke redshirted in 1991 and first saw varsity
action as a redshirt freshman during the 1992 season as

a reserve wingback. "Words can't describe how I felt the first time I walked into the stadium in a Nebraska uniform. All of the red and the noise...it left me speechless. Just standing on the sidelines during the game was really quite a thrill for me in the beginning," explained Schmadeke. During the upcoming spring football practice, Schmadeke moved from wingback to defensive back.

"At Albion I pretty much ran the ball and didn't do much receiving. I always had doubts about my hands and catching ability and it showed during practice. I dropped some balls. Just when I was getting ready to request a position change, the coaches came to me and said they thought I could help in the secondary."

The move proved to be a positive one for Schmadeke. Entering the 1993 campaign, he was listed third on the depth chart. "I was one player away from traveling to the UCLA game. I was thrilled," said Schmadeke. The 1993 season and 1994 Orange Bowl game proved to be a thrill. "It was great to be affiliated with the team. We gained some respect and I feel that loss was a major turning point in Nebraska football history. Who knows, had we not lost that game, we might not have had the drive to go back-to-back," said Schmadeke. As it turned out, the Huskers and Schmadeke were more than ready for the 1994 season. Unfortunately, Schmadeke's brother Damon did not see the football field again as a player after suffering a serious back injury. Damon missed his final two seasons of football eligibility and was relegated to serve as an undergraduate assistant coach.

Darren Schmadeke opened the 1994 season as the backup left cornerback to Jim Thorpe candidate Barron Miles. "Barron was great to play behind. He gave me confidence that helped me get the job done," recalled Schmadeke. Making the Nebraska travel roster was a milestone in Schmadeke's Nebraska career. "I never thought I would travel with the team other than to bowl games. To make the travel squad as a junior and go to every game was a huge accomplishment." In Nebraska's fourth game, against Pacific, Schmadeke got the chance to showcase his talents. "I played all four quarters and led the team with eight tackles. I was glad to have the opportunity to play that much. It really boosted my confidence." Nebraska cruised to a 70-21 win.

"That '94 season was kind of like a fairy tale with a perfect finish. The team was confident that we would win the title." Schmadeke's reaction after Nebraska's 24-17 come-from-behind Orange Bowl win against Miami: "I really couldn't take it all in in that moment. Words can't describe how I felt. I'll never forget being a part of that team."

In addition to being a member of the Nebraska football "fraternity," Darren and his brother were both Farmhouse Fraternity members. "We became members right away as freshmen. I personally found it to be a very positive experience. It was important for me to be more than a football player. I was able to develop a wide variety of friendships with guys who had similar goals and interests. It's difficult to describe the brotherhood you feel in a fraternity until you have been a member," remarked Schmadeke.

After claiming the national title in 1994, Schmadeke's fraternity brothers and fans nationwide began speculating if Nebraska could repeat. "I really believed we had a legitimate shot to win the whole thing again. The way Frazier was clicking at the end of the Orange Bowl, and knowing the returning talent we had, I think our whole team was very confident."

After impressive bowl performances against Florida State and Miami in back-to-back Orange Bowls, people weren't nearly as critical of the secondary. "It seemed like Coach George Darlington and the secondary were taking lots of criticism. I think there were a couple of key turning points. We were recruiting the very best athletes to play in the secondary and the coaches installed some pro defensive packages with zone blitzes. We would move up and back and really fool the quarterback into making some big mistakes," said Schmadeke.

Schmadeke is convinced the Huskers' strong team unity was the ultimate factor in helping the Huskers stay focused and on-track for a repeat bid to claim the coveted national championship. "Winning the title again was our only way to show the nation that our program was in check and we could still be successful despite the distractions." When he first made the decision to become a Husker, Schmadeke never imagined leaving the program with five Big Eight championship rings and two national championship rings. "I thought maybe a couple Big Eight titles would be pretty amazing. Going back-to-back probably won't set in for years to come. I'm sure down the road my grandchildren will be hearing stories about my Nebraska career, especially the interception I made against Missouri to preserve a 57-0 shutout," said Schmadeke.

Schmadeke credits the Nebraska experience with much more than adding to his jewelry collection. "Nebraska football taught me lessons of life. I started at the bottom and did the little things day in and day out just to get a chance. This is a cycle I expect to go through over and over in life. In the end, I know lots of people respect me for sticking it out and playing a small part on a team that some call the greatest ever."

As for his future, after he graduates in May of 1996: "I'm applying to veterinary school and other graduate programs. I might even begin full-time employment with my father's insurance agency," said Schmadeke.

41

PHIL
ELLIS

Nebraska football coaches have a knack for discovering talent. First impressions of linebacker Phil Ellis probably wouldn't stack up against those of most major college football prospects. Rarely would there be hoopla and fanfare over the eventual team co-captain, four-year letter winner and 1995 honorable mention All-Big Eight selection, but what matters to Ellis are the final impressions he left on the Nebraska program.

Born and raised in Grand Island, Nebraska, his mother and stepfather divorced when he was in the fifth grade. Phil then moved with his mother to Albuquerque, New Mexico. "We were there for about a year and a half and then we moved to North Dakota. I didn't like moving around; it was hard to make new friends all of the time," recalled Ellis. Longing to return to Nebraska, Ellis moved back to Grand Island and lived with his stepfather and older brother. "At the time, it was really hard to leave my mother because she always did the best for me. Her career required travel and relocation and at that time a move back to Nebraska seemed in my best interest," remembered Ellis.

"My stepfather was a trucker so he was out on the road most of the time. My brother and I pretty much took care of ourselves. Obviously, it wasn't an ideal situation and my mother realized that. She wanted us to move in with our aunt and uncle who also lived in Grand Island," remembered Ellis, then in the ninth grade. Not crazy about yet another move, Ellis acknowledged eventually warming up to Aunt Shirley and Uncle Ron. "We became real close and it turned out to be a very good situation in terms of growth and stability."

Early on during his high school career at Grand Island High School, people began telling Ellis he was a talented athlete. "In my junior year, Nebraska called and invited me to the Oklahoma game. I knew I had always wanted to be a Husker but hadn't put much thought into college. Honestly, I was somewhat surprised that Nebraska showed an interest in me," recalled Ellis. Excited about the early interest Nebraska had expressed in him, Ellis attended the Big Red Football School the summer prior to his senior year. During the camp, Nebraska told Ellis he would be offered a full athletic scholarship. "I was shocked. I thanked Coach Osborne and told him I would stay in touch. I tried to downplay the emotion and frankly, still didn't see what the coaches saw in me."

Ellis gave his verbal commitment in August to Coach Osborne before the start of his high school senior season. "I wanted to return the favor to Nebraska. They showed early interest in me and I knew Nebraska was the place for me. There was no need for me to tease them and take other visits," explained Ellis. There were many factors that made Nebraska an easy choice for Ellis. "Number one was the winning tradition and second was their reputation for developing the total person."

Despite his early commitment, other schools continued to pursue Ellis. "Sure it was an honor and a boost to my ego but I never wavered." Upon making his commitment to the Big Red, Ellis became a celebrity of sorts in Grand Island. "I was doing lots of interviews with the media but was looking forward to things settling down so I could go out in style my senior year," said Ellis. He went out in style, earning every high school honor imaginable and helping lead his team to state runner-up in Class A.

Going from being on top of the football world as a talented high school senior to being a new, undersized freshman football player at one of the top football programs in the country can be a tough adjustment. "I lacked muscle and size and can vividly remember seeing Christian Peter. He weighed 320 pounds and suddenly my confidence was nonexistent. He looked like an animal. I did take some comfort finding out he was also on defense," said Ellis. "I was scared at first and really didn't know what to expect or if I was out of my league." A really rude awakening was in store when the varsity reported to fall camp. "It was really rough and intense and a feeling I kept with me throughout my Nebraska career. Whenever a new freshman class would come in, I would always try to remember my feelings at that time. As a result I tried to be more of a mentor than an intimidator," recalled Ellis.

Ellis considered the strong unity among the linebackers as extremely helpful in his adjustment to college life and Nebraska Football. "Guys like Mike Anderson, Darren Williams, Troy Branch and I developed special friendships. Williams and Branch shared their backgrounds and what life experiences they'd had. These guys beat the inner-city odds. Lincoln looked really good to some of those guys compared to the things they saw on a daily basis." Ellis felt like he could connect with the players who had come from different backgrounds and risen to the top. "I've been through two divorces and they were really hard on me. Those experiences made me a tougher person emotionally and I certainly feel for guys who are going through rough family or personal problems."

Ellis relied on his emotional stability and will power to survive the difficult freshman year. After a year as a redshirt, the intense yet modest Ellis was ready to return to competition. As a redshirt freshman in 1992, Ellis saw considerable action on special teams and played in all but one game. "Special teams can be a guy's ticket to proving himself. Special teams are lots of fun and a great way to get on the field and maybe even make the travel squad," explained Ellis.

"Taking the field at Memorial Stadium the first time, I walked out with two guys, Brook Berringer and Aaron Graham who later became my roommates. It was just crazy and I remember looking up into the crowd and being in total awe. I was still in a daze when I was on the field for the opening kickoff. I wanted to run down the field and do something special. That was a feeling I had every time I took the field," said Ellis.

In retrospect, Ellis surpassed his expectations. "I traveled as a redshirt freshman and was playing with the big boys right away. Everything that happened to me that year reinforced the values of hard work and commitment. I'm a prime example because although

I'm far from the fastest or strongest, I still proved I could get the job done," said Ellis. "Lots of great athletes come through Nebraska who never see the field because they don't work hard." Ellis also credits the Nebraska football experience for helping him mature as a man. "The coaches at Nebraska try to teach life lessons and get players prepared for the real world. I learned the importance of teamwork and unity to reach goals," acknowledged Ellis.

As a redshirt sophomore, Ellis continued to excel. Quickly becoming regarded as one of Nebraska's most valuable special teams players, he continued to back up linebackers Ed Stewart, Mike Anderson and Troy Branch. "My playing time gradually increased and so did my confidence. The 'mike' linebacker is like being the quarterback of the defense and requires great concentration, smarts and mental composure," added Ellis.

Ellis and the Huskers needed all of the composure they could muster after losing the national championship to Florida State in the 1994 Orange Bowl game. "We had a really good team that year and, even though the loss was disappointing, we all walked off that field with our heads held high. I feel we outplayed them and were the better team. I think the nation knew it and even some of the Seminoles probably agree we deserved to win," concluded Ellis.

Although the Huskers lost the game, they won the national respect the team had been longing for. "We knew we could play with the big boys; the Florida teams which were so explosive and intimidating all of a sudden didn't seem unbeatable. We now had confidence that we could be in the position to play for the title every year, and we were determined not to let another national championship get away." Hence, the slogan the Huskers would live by for the next year, *Unfinished Business.*

According to Ellis, the Huskers game plan to "finish business" began in the off-season and the summer before the 1994 season. "All the guys stayed around during the summer, and we became unified as a team with a common goal," recalled Ellis. Team unity ultimately played a critical role in the Huskers' quest for the school's first national crown since 1971. "When Frazier went down, I became a little concerned, but I knew what Brook could do. Brook's biggest disadvantage was his lack of experience. Experience makes all the difference in the world, and I think everyone saw Brook's confidence rise with each game." With the steady and sometimes spectacular performance of Berringer and stellar defensive efforts, Ellis felt the national championship was still be a reality. "Our defense was clicking; I had no doubts and the team had a one-track mind in regard to the title," said Ellis who was splitting time with Doug Colman at the starting "mike" linebacker position during his junior year.

Ellis and the Husker blackshirts had an attitude throughout the '94 championship drive. "The way the defense looked at it, we determined the outcome of the game. If the opponent didn't score, they weren't going to win the game. We absolutely hated giving up points and wanted the goose egg every time," recalled Ellis, who took over the starting role from the Colorado game on. "It all comes back to unity. You play as a team and you win as a team."

The Huskers proved Ellis's point during the 1995 Orange Bowl against the University of Miami. "Everybody chipped in and did what was necessary for us to win. We were the number one team in the nation, and Miami had to come and take it from us." Ellis felt honored to be part of such a memorable contest. "It was a great game and I was biting my nails. By the third quarter we could sense the game was ours," explained Ellis. "Even though we were still behind, you could see Miami getting fatigued. We came up with big play after big play on defense and knew it was just a matter of time before the offense would click. That game was so much fun to be a part of, especially our last defensive stand. There was no doubt we would get to Costa every time. I remember going up and hugging guys like Christian, Connealy and Donta after every play."

When the final gun went off and the Gatorade came flying, all emotions were unleashed. "The monkey was suddenly off everyone's back. Winning the national championship was a great thing, but there were so many other victories within the victory," said Ellis. "Suddenly Tom Osborne was a genius. The Huskers proved they could beat a Florida school. They could win on grass in the Orange Bowl and beat high-powered passing attacks. All of those factors combined made it such a special win for everyone involved."

Shortly after winning the 1994 National Championship, the Huskers zeroed in on the goal of a repeat. "We definitely felt that was a realistic goal. I think some teams list the national championship as a team goal because it's the ultimate goal to shoot for. The national championship was a goal we fully expected to reach," said

Ellis. "Our attitude was, 'Hey, we are the national champions until someone can come and take it from us!'"

As the 1995 season unfolded, opponents were focused on stealing the trophy while others were determined to tear down the Nebraska program. One of five team captains for the 1995 Huskers, Ellis and his co-captains played a pivotal role in keeping the Huskers on course for a date with history.

With his selection as a team captain, Ellis was both stunned and honored. "We had so many great people and capable leaders. The fact that five captains were selected for the first time in school history tells you something about the quality of our seniors." Ellis identified his leadership on and off the field, as well as a good old-fashioned work ethic, as the positive attributes others saw in him. "From the day I was told I was a captain, I held my chin a little bit higher. I tried to be a good listener and be a voice for the seniors and the entire team."

Once again the starter at "mike" linebacker, Ellis also had a voice in the defensive huddle. "I was basically the quarterback of the defense and responsible for calling the plays. I tried to rely on good psychology during the tough times to keep everyone in the game," said Ellis. "For example, if a defensive back got beat deep, then in the huddle I would challenge the up-front guys to get a better pass-rush in hopes of redirecting the attention and not putting blame on anyone," recalled Ellis.

Later on, Ellis, who earned his degree in biological sciences in a four-and-a-half year period, was called upon again to employ his psychological tactics. "After the Phillips incident occurred, the team captains got together to talk about our goals being at risk. At first we overreacted with some unrealistic and strict rules. Then we decided to have a players-only meeting," remembered Ellis. "The captains talked about how the most respected coach in the country was being torn down before our eyes and that each of us needed to refocus his efforts." The team channeled their energy to the playing field. "Our frustration with the media scrutiny was reflected in our actions on the field. We wanted to play flawlessly, forcing the writers to shift their stories to great football and not dwell on past negatives that most of us had no part of. Ultimately, we knew we couldn't influence the media but we could stay focused and take care of business," continued Ellis.

Ellis, who was married in January, 1996 to the former Jennifer Jardine, is regarded as a soft-spoken and mild-mannered person. The negative media portrayal of Tom Osborne throughout the 1995 season angered Ellis and his teammates. "Tom Osborne is the most honest, caring man I know. He cares so much about every player from the scout team to starter and he always has an open door policy if we need to discuss any concerns. It really angered me to see people question his judgment and decisions."

Ellis was convinced the extreme scrutiny had an up side. "I think everyone within the program matured and learned important lessons, including Lawrence Phillips. I remember one day in the weight room he came up to me and told me how much it meant to him that Coach Osborne and the team stuck by him. That whole situation definitely motivated us to finish the job and prove to the nation that we had the character to pull together through tough situations and not miss a beat."

Ellis, however did miss a few beats due to a fractured right foot that caused him to sit out four games. Ellis was back for the Colorado game, made some huge plays in the Kansas game and won back his starting job for the season finale against Oklahoma. "The shutout victory was a great way to end my home career and best of all it put us back where we wanted to be, in the national championship game," said Ellis.

Again, Ellis relied upon sound psychology to help give the Huskers an edge in the 1996 Fiesta Bowl. "At all of the pre-game press conferences, our players always complimented the Florida team and commented on how dangerous and explosive they were. We kept repeating that so our opponents would read the papers and think they were better than they really were. We tried to set them up through the media." According to Ellis, the players and coaches were supremely confident about their chances. "I was so ready for that game! I mentally prepared for a week. Obviously when I found myself watching the game on the sidelines in the third quarter, it was a little bit of a letdown," said Ellis.

In the thrill of victory and back-to-back national championships, Ellis was quick to empathize with the Florida team. "I knew how they felt because we went through that same helpless feeling with the Miami loss in 1993. You could just see it in their faces and I think the experience of playing in a national championship game will help them in coming years," explained Ellis. He also expressed regret that the players who were seniors on the 1993 Husker team couldn't be awarded a national championship ring. "Those guys like Trev Alberts, Troy Branch, Corey Dixon and all of the others built the tradition and that one Florida State loss shifted everything. I feel we owe them something and I'm sure deep down they know they played a big part in our success," said Ellis.

In the days following the Fiesta Bowl win, Ellis was frequently asked which championship was better. "They were both the best and each had its own special moments and memories." Although, Ellis said he felt more connected to the 1995 crown. "Winning — being a senior and team captain and with the team being up against many odds — was really a special way to hang up my Nebraska helmet."

Football may be over for Phil Ellis and although that saddens him, his biggest concern is maintaining relationships. "I hope we all keep in touch and have some special national championship reunions. Football has been the major thing in my life for the past five years. It is hard to imagine not going through the same routines that dominated my college life." Ellis is convinced that life beyond Nebraska will be a positive one and credits the Nebraska experience for his optimism. "I came here thinking I wouldn't even sniff the playing field and really had doubts about myself. But, if given the chance and if you work hard, dreams can come true!"

PHOTO BY DENNIS HUBBARD

46

DOUG COLMAN

If there was ever a person destined to be a football player, Doug Colman fits the profile. His father, Wayne, played in the National Football League for both the Philadelphia Eagles and the New Orleans Saints. The elder Colman played linebacker in the league for nine years, walking away from the game on his own terms in 1977. Even with his father's football background, Doug Colman was never forced into the game.

"The way my father tells it, when I was two years old, some people tried to get me playing in a league for five year olds. I was well developed compared to others my age, but come on, age two?" Colman fought off the early recruiters until age seven when he became active with the Ventnor Pirates, a Pop Warner football team. The Ventnor, New Jersey, native went on to play football through his teen years and has especially vivid memories of his Pop Warner experience. "I remember wearing red and white and tackling a guy, knocking the ball loose and running for a touchdown. I felt like I was on the top of the world," said Colman.

In the beginning, football was nothing more than a hobby for Colman and a way to run off energy. "It was

was the sport of choice in my neighborhood, and I only did it to get involved and fit in with the other kids." As time evolved, Colman followed his father's footsteps and became a highly-touted prep standout. At Ocean City High School, Colman showcased his athleticism, excelling at both linebacker and fullback. The South Jersey area got a sneak preview of Colman's ability during his freshman year. "They only let freshmen suit up for the Thanksgiving Day game and I played in the second through the fourth quarters. I had a good game and that really set the tone for the rest of my high school career," remarked Colman.

During his junior and senior high school years, Colman had the opportunity to play for his father who became the school's head coach. "That was a good experience. I really respected the way my father coached. He was a teacher on the field and able to motivate people in a special way. I played the games for my father because I wanted to make him proud," said Colman. Having a father as a coach produced some interesting situations. "As the linebacker I took the signals from the sidelines and called the defensive plays. If I had a feeling a different call would work, on occasion I would overrule my Dad and, of course, that didn't always go over well. I heard about it when I came off the field."

As Colman's high school days continued, he rarely left the field playing for the red and white clad Ocean City High School team. "They tried me at fullback and the first time I carried the ball I ran 40-some yards for a touchdown. Fullback was OK but my heart was really

at the linebacker position." Colman went on to earn
All-State and All-South Jersey honors at linebacker and
was the 1990 South Jersey defensive player-of-the-year.
He also earned All-County honors at the fullback position. Colman appeared on track to following his father's footsteps to the National Football League. Prior
to the end of his senior season, college recruiters nationwide were calling on the Colman household.

"The recruiting got so intense, my parents decided
no more coaches were allowed to visit our home,"
recalled Colman. Rutgers showed early and consistent
interest; however, Colman was determined to become
a part of a tradition-rich and top-ranked program. "In
the beginning, I was thinking Virginia, Penn State,
Michigan or Michigan State. Virginia and Michigan State
were really the frontrunners until Coach Frank Solich
and Dr. Tom Osborne entered the picture. Nebraska's
Coach Solich called and indicated he was in the area
and wanted to stop by. He knew I didn't have all of
my official visits scheduled; he eventually persuaded
me to at least look at the campus." During Colman's
senior year, Nebraska's head coach made a visit to
Colman's high school. "Someone came to my classroom and was all excited that Coach Tom Osborne was
in the office and wanted to see me. I really didn't know
who he was and was far from awe-struck. I do remember being very impressed by his non-threatening de-
meanor and how easy he was to talk with."

Colman eventually decided to visit the University
of Nebraska-Lincoln and was favorably impressed.
"Linebacker Mike Anderson from Grand Island was my

host. It was clear there was a lot of team unity and support for the student athletes. Still, I wasn't ready to make my decision, but the fact that Nebraska was recruiting me mainly as a linebacker was appealing to me. I also felt Nebraska would give me the best chance and the most exposure to make it at the next level," said Colman. His decision became solidified after a series of phone calls one week before the signing date from the Michigan State and Nebraska coaching staffs.

"Michigan State called and told me that if I didn't make a decision soon, my scholarship wouldn't be available and it would go to someone else. They were putting some definite pressure on me and I was really taken back by all that. Coach Osborne handled matters without pressure. He said that he realized I was looking at very good schools and that this was one of the most important decisions I would ever make. He stressed taking my time and said that even if I decided after the signing date, a scholarship would still be available for me."

Osborne's approach proved to be the difference for Colman. "Coach Osborne recruited in a very positive way. He did not talk negatively about other schools and when he said they would hold a scholarship for me while I was deciding, I knew then that Nebraska thought a lot of me." Colman remembers when Coach Frank Solich of Nebraska called one week before the national letter of intent signing day. "His call came immediately after the high-pressure pitch from Michigan State. I immediately asked Coach Solich if they had number 46 in red and white. He said 'yes' and I said 'yes,'" remarked Colman.

Relieved that he made his decision on where to attend college and continue his football career, Colman endured some negative backlash on his decision to leave the east coast. "Rutgers was really upset that I was leaving the state but eventually they told me if I ever got homesick and wanted to return to Jersey to keep them in mind."

Upon his arrival in Lincoln, Nebraska, during the summer of 1991, Colman was optimistic he could play for the Huskers as a true freshman. "I just couldn't imagine being without football for a year. During the recruitment process, the coaches had told me they felt I could play right away," explained Colman. Things were off to a great start for Colman until the varsity reported. "I remember being in drills and lining up across from linebacker Darren Williams who was known as one of our fiercest hitters. I think linebacker coach Kevin Steele leaned over to Darren and told him something like, 'that rookie is trying to take your job!' Darren nailed me so hard that my nose 'blew up.' I stumbled backwards and blood was everywhere. I took off my helmet and I had double vision. All the guys asked me if I was OK and I said 'Wow! I just got rocked.'" Colman sat out the remainder of practice and it wasn't until later that night that his vision returned to normal.

Colman's early memories about Nebraska football included being surprised at the number of players. "We had 20-some linebackers and a football field full of players. Even though I had confidence in my abilities, I was definitely overwhelmed," said Colman. Nevertheless, Colman made a quick adjustment to big time college football.

Colman was one of three true freshmen to suit up and letter in 1991. Safety Troy Dumas and wingback Abdul Muhammad were the other two Huskers to bypass redshirt years. Colman entered his freshman season as fourth on the depth chart at weak-side linebacker and wore number 28, not his lucky high school number 46. "Troy Dumas wore number 46 and the funny thing about it was he didn't even want it." At that point, the jersey number was not an issue. Colman was caught up in the excitement of playing as a true freshman. What was significant for Colman was the first time he walked out of the locker room into Memorial Stadium.

"I started crying like I'd never cried before. I was so juiced up to go I just couldn't stop crying. Of course, as a football player, I had to try to hide it and not let the other players see me getting all teary-eyed. The crowd, the red and the excitement was something I could have never been prepared for," said Colman. Colman wasn't on the travel roster as a true freshman and ended up playing in five games at reserve linebacker and on special teams. "The away games were tough but in looking back it allowed me to expand my friendships. I got to know some of the older guys who didn't travel and I developed what proved to be some long-lasting friendships," explained Colman.

On his decision to play as a true freshman, Colman had some regrets. "I felt like I didn't contribute as
much as I would have liked and lost a year of my
career without much to show for it." As Colman's career unfolded, he, like many other players, learned to
redefine his individual goals and become focused on
the bigger picture — conference and national championships.

Re-evaluating his goals upon arriving at Nebraska,
Colman still thought it was realistic to start two years
for Nebraska. Still behind middle linebackers Mike Anderson, Darren Williams and Ed Stewart on the depth
chart, Colman was leaning toward a redshirt year in
1992. According to Colman, the coaching staff wanted
him available on the sidelines in the event of injury to
some of the top players.

"We negotiated a compromise. Coach Osborne
told me if anyone got hurt before the sixth game of the
season I would not redshirt. Up to that point, I would
dress out and be available. Naturally, I was hoping
there would be no major injuries at linebacker because
that would mean I would use another year and at the
most get five or six games," explained Colman. During
week six of the 1992 campaign Colman found out his
father would be in Lincoln for the weekend. "I asked
Coach Steele if I could sit in the stands with my father.
He was reluctant at first but eventually agreed. During
the course of the game linebacker Mike Anderson got
hurt and had to come out. Matt Penland went in and
on his first play he broke his leg and blew his knee out
all at once. Had I been in uniform, I would have been

in the game and there would have been no redshirt year."

As a result of various position changes and the blackshirts switching to a 4-3 defense, Colman was able to preserve his redshirt year. "I was relieved to have the redshirt year and I felt it was the best thing for me and the team in the long run," said Colman.

As a redshirt sophomore and wearing number 46, Colman was coming off his best spring ball. He felt like he was in contention for major minutes behind starter Mike Anderson at middle linebacker. "I became good friends with some of the older linebackers and felt like I might have let friendships get in the way of position battles. I regret having that mentality at the time and later realized that frame of mind was holding me back." Colman still managed to play in all eleven regular season games and the 1994 Orange Bowl. "I got into the Bowl game in the second quarter — I was so intense and ready to play. I knew everyone back home would be watching me and I wanted our team to play well." In one of his first plays, he had the chance to sack Heisman Trophy winner Charlie Ward of Florida State. "As I was bearing down on Ward, part of me was asking myself, 'Who am I? That's Heisman winner Charlie Ward and I'm Doug Colman.' I ended up running him out of bounds. At that point, I realized that I couldn't feel inferior to anyone on the field or I wouldn't be successful."

Even though Nebraska wasn't successful on the scoreboard against Florida State, Colman was far from discouraged after the heartbreaking defeat. "Everyone gave it their all and even though we lost, I think all of the players and coaches felt fulfilled and encouraged. Some guys were crying in the locker room, but I couldn't. I was proud of the effort and determined to play an even bigger role in the upcoming year," said Colman.

Heading into his junior year during the 1994 season, Colman was still working to achieve his goal of being a two-year starter for the Husker blackshirts. Before his work began on the field, he and fellow New Jersey native and defensive tackle Christian Peter went to work on their teammates. "We had the chance to play in either the Pigskin Classic in Anaheim, California, or the Kickoff Classic in New Jersey, at the Meadowlands. Christian and I persuaded the majority of the team to vote 'no' for the Pigskin Classic and 'yes' to the Kickoff Classic. I was so excited to have the chance to return to Jersey and play in Giants Stadium."

Colman's trip east became more meaningful after he earned a starting position at the "mike" linebacker spot. "I had over one hundred family and friends in attendance, including several guys from my high school. I was ready to show everyone my talent and prove that I was a big-time player." Colman did just that! He recorded a career high eight tackles, including one 10-yard sack and one other tackle for a loss. Colman also caused and recovered a fumble in Nebraska's 31-0 victory over twenty-fourth ranked West Virginia. "It was a storybook homecoming for me. After the game, I saw my family and became really emotional. I felt like that game wiped out some of my previous struggles," explained Colman.

Even though Colman started the next seven games for the Huskers on their road to the national championship, he was constantly being challenged by Grand Island, Nebraska, native Phil Ellis. "Phil was always creeping up on me and was getting more and more time in each game. I was committed to being a team player and making good on our goal to 'finish business.'" During the ninth game against Colorado, the coaching staff opted to start Phil Ellis at "mike" linebacker. "I was disappointed because many of my family and friends were in for the game. Still, I gave it my all when I was in the game and put up some big numbers," remarked Colman.

While Nebraska and the entire college football world were caught up in the Husker quarterback situation with the injuries of Tommie Frazier and Brook Berringer, Colman and Ellis were locked in a battle for the starting position that continued for the rest of their careers. Ellis started the final five games of the 1994 season including the 1995 Orange Bowl game. Colman and the blackshirts came up huge, stifling the Hurricanes in the fourth quarter. "The victory was great because I really felt a part of it. My real joy came for Coach Osborne because everyone said Miami would destroy us. We were all just tired of the lack of respect being shown to Coach Osborne and the entire program," said Colman.

Colman recalls a discussion he had during his senior year with top "mike" linebacker contender, Phil

Ellis. "We both made a pact to give it our best and be supportive. We were convinced that everything would have a way of working out. The 6-3, 245-pound senior started the 1995 season as the backup to Ellis for the first four games. Prior to the Washington State game, Ellis broke his foot in practice and Colman was called upon to start the next six games. Nebraska didn't miss a beat in the transition. Colman lived up to the confidence of the coaches, especially against Colorado and Kansas State.

Heading into the last Big Eight Conference game in the history of the league — against arch-rival Oklahoma — Nebraska position coach Craig Bohl was forced to choose between the healed Ellis and the capable Colman for the starting position. "I had prepared myself for the possibility that Phil would be named the starter and I was going to be supportive of the coach's decision," said Colman. Ellis was tabbed the starter for the Oklahoma game; Colman, though disappointed, readily accepted the decision.

The Huskers were in the midst of national scrutiny as a result of some off-the-field incidents involving high profile players. "During all of the adversity, the team made a commitment to be totally unified, to step-up our intensity and to play for Coach Osborne. I have the utmost respect for Coach Osborne — the way he supports his players through good and bad. He could have taken the easy way out and dismissed some guys from the team, but he did what he felt would be best for the person behind the player," concluded Colman. "Playing for Coach Tom Osborne was a great honor. He takes special interest in each of his players. If I came back ten years from now, he would remember everything about me and ask about my parents by their first names," said Colman.

When it came time for the 1996 Fiesta Bowl, the Huskers were full of motivation. "We wanted to silence all the doubters and help make a statement to the nation on behalf of Coach Osborne. I felt we accomplished that goal with one of the most complete games ever played under those circumstances." Colman figured prominently in a second quarter safety scored by Husker backer Jamel Williams. "It was a busted play. Tony Veland swears he gave me the coverage call but I don't remember getting it. At the last minute, I saw the back go into motion and signaled for a blitz. Jamel came clean and sacked Wuerffel for a deuce," recalled Colman.

Reflecting on his Husker career, Colman's record surpassed all his expectations. "We were a bunch of no-name guys, ranked 30-something as a recruiting class. But you can't measure heart and drive. Coupled with team unity those things allowed us to make history," summarized Colman. Ecstatic with the team accomplishments, Colman feels like there is still plenty of good football left in him. "I believe I can play at the next level and that I'm a hidden commodity. National Football League teams like my strength, speed and size. I'm just hoping for an opportunity to show my talent."

In the event football isn't in Colman's future, he intends to stay connected with athletics. A secondary education major, Colman is preparing to teach physical education and coach football. "I've had some great coaching role models in my life and would like nothing better than to give back to youngsters." Colman would incorporate aspects of both his father's and Coach Osborne's coaching philosophy into his own style. "I would be a motivator, but would understand the special needs of individuals," said Colman.

As part of the Nebraska football program, Colman was quick to modify individual dreams for team unity. Undoubtedly, he has the talent to fulfill either of his goals — playing in the National Football League or becoming a great educator and coach.

The 1994 Season

Nebraska	31	West Virginia	0
Nebraska	42	Texas Tech	16
Nebraska	49	UCLA	21
Nebraska	70	Pacific	21
Nebraska	42	Wyoming	32
Nebraska	32	Oklahoma State	3
Nebraska	17	Kansas State	6
Nebraska	42	Missouri	7
Nebraska	24	Colorado	7
Nebraska	45	Kansas	17
Nebraska	28	Iowa State	12
Nebraska	13	Oklahoma	3

Orange Bowl

Nebraska	24	Miami	17

Team Statistics

(12 regular season games)

Category	NU	Opp.
First downs	293.0	176.0
Total Yards	5,734.0	3,106.0
Avg. per game	477.8	258.8
Net Rushing Yards	4,080.0	951.0
Avg. per game	340.0	79.3
Net passing yards	1,654.0	2,155.0
Avg. per game	137.8	179.6
Total Points	435.0	145.0
Avg. per game	36.3	12.1

The Rush

The thrill of entering Memorial Stadium was felt by each player on football Saturday.

The Coach

Coach Tom Osborne and Christian Peter shared some special times in the '95 season.

Tom Osborne & Tony Veland prior to '95 Oklahoma game.

Coaches Tom Osborne and Ron Brown call plays from the sideline.

The Captains

Cornhusker captains preparing for the coin toss. Left to right: Christian Peter, Phil Ellis, Tony Veland, Mark Gilman. Below is Aaron Graham.

Nebraska had five captains during the '95 season rather than the usual four.

UN-L PHOTOGRAPHY BY RICHARD VOGES

PHOTO BY DENNIS HUBBARD

The Quarterbacks

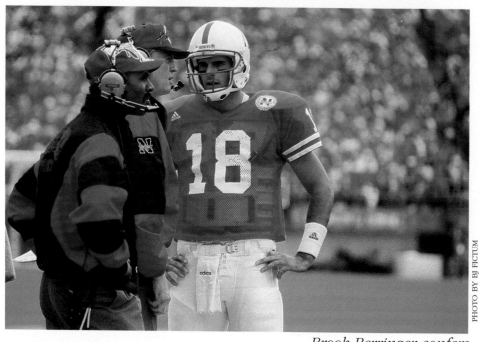

Brook Berringer confers with Coaches Tom Osborne and Ron Brown before entering the game.

First Team All-American Tommie Fraizer broke many records and won honors in the four seasons that he started as quarterback for Nebraska.

The Game

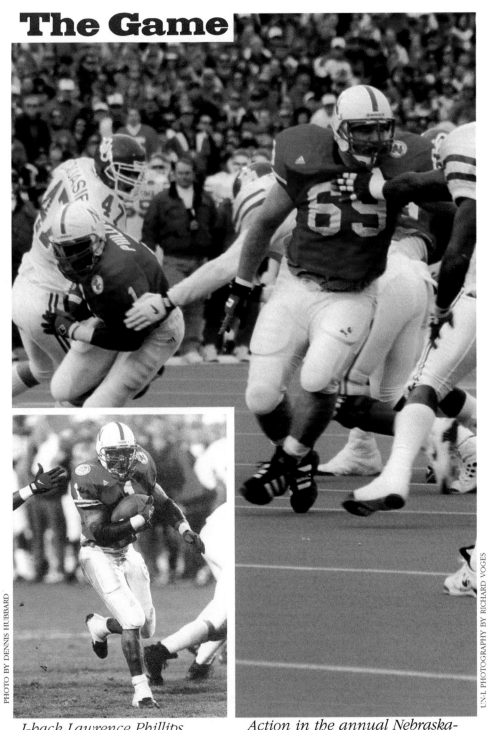

I-back Lawrence Phillips in one of the many great runs in the '96 Fiesta Bowl.

Action in the annual Nebraska-Oklahoma clash shows right guard Steve Ott defending Lawrence Phillips' run.

The Fans

PHOTO BY DENNIS HUBBARD

UN-L PHOTOGRAPHY By ...

The Media

Linebackers Aaron Penland and Phil Ellis joke with ESPN Sportscaster Lee Corso.

Lawrence Phillips responding to questions from the national media prior to the 1996 Fiesta Bowl.

The Championship

ANOTHER
BIG 8
CHAMPIONSHIP
HUSKERS #1

The 1995 Season

Nebraska	64	Oklahoma State	21
Nebraska	50	Michigan State	10
Nebraska	77	Arizona State	28
Nebraska	49	Pacific	7
Nebraska	35	Washington State	21
Nebraska	57	Missouri	0
Nebraska	49	Kansas State	25
Nebraska	44	Colorado	21
Nebraska	62	Iowa State	14
Nebraska	41	Kansas	3
Nebraska	37	Oklahoma	0

Fiesta Bowl

| Nebraska | 62 | Florida | 24 |

Team Statistics

(11 regular season games)

Category	NU	Opp.
First downs	298.0	170.0
Total Yards	6,119.0	3,235.0
Avg. per game	556.3	294.0
Net Rushing Yards	4,398.0	862.0
Avg. per game	399.8	78.3
Net Passing Yards	1,721.0	2,373.0
Avg. per game	156.4	215.7
Total Points	576.0	150.0
Avg. per game	52.3	13.6

52

AARON PENLAND

Husker linebacker Aaron Penland is a man of true convictions. Penland sacrificed a full scholarship at Liberty University in Lynchburg, Virginia, to walk-on at Nebraska. "I didn't want to look back and have any regrets. I knew I could play at the Division I level and was determined to be successful," explained Penland. The doubters said Penland was too small to play major college football. "I wanted to prove people wrong. Lots of guys will talk big, but I was ready to walk the walk," said Penland.

By making the decision to come to Nebraska, Penland got the opportunity to play with his older brother, Matt. Matt Penland played linebacker for the Huskers in 1992 and 1993 before injury terminated his playing career; he concluded his tenure as a student-assistant coach.

Aaron redshirted in 1991 and came to rely upon his faith in Christ and the support of his brother to make it through a challenging year. "Matt knew the ropes and introduced me to many of his friends. He definitely made the transition much easier for me," remarked Penland. After making it through his redshirt season, Penland was excited for the start of the 1992 season.

Penland knew that as a walk-on he had to be at the top of his game at all times in order to catch the attention of the NU coaching staff. "I felt I had to prove myself every day and give 100 percent at all times. There was definitely a sense of pressure to perform at every practice." Penland responded to the pressure — he played in eight games during the 1992 campaign. "I would do anything I possibly could to get on the field." In fact, Penland negotiated with outside linebacker Donta Jones with the goal of getting the chance to play more on kickoff teams. "Donta always played quite a bit as backup rush end. I told him I was fresh and could step in for him on kickoffs. Donta rarely argued and usually told the coaches that he preferred not to be a regular on kickoffs when he was in the rush rotation."

Penland succeeded in his bid to catch the attention of the Husker coaching staff. Prior to the end of the season, Penland made the travel roster. "I got moved up right before the Oklahoma game. To make the travel roster as a redshirt freshman was a major accomplishment. I really felt satisfied, as if I'd made a contribution to the success of the team." Penland started on the kickoff team for both the Oklahoma game and the Coca-Cola Bowl in Tokyo against Kansas State. But, Penland did more than make a contribution to the Huskers, he set a daily example for his teammates.

At 6-1, 225 pounds, Penland was regarded by his peers as a stable, dedicated and hard-working player who always gave 110 percent. On special teams, Penland drew praise for his intensity and all-out hustle. Penland quickly joined the ranks of the so-called "wedge-breakers." Penland and others were charged with the duty of breaking through the wedge created by the opposing kick-return team. Penland had the toughness to be a great wedge-breaker and by some accounts, he had the proper mentality as well. "Some of the guys say you have to be a little bit 'out there' to be a good special teams player. Whatever the case, I've always enjoyed playing special teams and used the experience as a stepping stone of sorts," explained Penland.

In 1993, Penland was a sophomore and optomistic about the season. But the year turned out to be bittersweet. Aaron was recovering from knee surgery and spent considerable time on the scout team. Through hard work and perseverance, Aaron was able to be on the field at the same time as his older brother Matt. "Those were great moments, very special." Unfortunately, later in the season, Matt Penland suffered a career-ending knee injury. "It was tough to see my brother experience such a devastating injury. We always shared both the good and bad times together." As a tribute to his older brother, Penland switched his jersey number to Matt's #52. By now, Penland had solidified his spot on special teams and also saw action at weak-side linebacker. Still, according to Penland, walk-ons can never relax. "I felt like

I always had to make my presence known and make certain everyone knew I was there to stay." Penland made his presence known on countless occasions.

"I remember once after practice I went back to my dorm room and suddenly couldn't remember anything. How did I get to my room? Where was my truck? Did I lock my locker?" Penland was able to phone his brother who immediately took him to the team trainers. "We had just finished seeing the trainers and I asked Matt...'When are we going to see the trainer?'" Penland, regarded as one of the most physical Husker hitters, had apparently suffered a concussion, causing him to lose his short-term memory. Despite occasional concussions and continual bouts with 300-pound offensive linemen, Penland showed steady improvement during his sophomore season and played in the 1994 Orange Bowl against Florida State.

"We didn't reach our goal of a national championship. I think we outplayed them and dominated them physically. It was good experience playing in a game of that magnitude. Our team became determined to get back to the title game in 1995," remarked Penland. Penland and the Huskers dedicated themselves to excellence in the off-season. "We developed a sense of unity by working out together everyday. We were very confident of a successful season," said Penland.

Unity and confidence were essential for the 1994 Husker team. Then, after losing quarterback Tommie Frazier to blood clots, Penland and the team never wavered in their quest for the championship. "I felt like we were 'on' every game. We were ready for Miami in the Orange Bowl and tried to put the so-called 'jinx' behind us." The confident Huskers eventually wore down the Hurricanes claiming a 24-17 win. Walk-on Aaron Penland was "walking-the-walk" — he was a force on special teams and backed up Butkus finalist Ed Stewart and Ryan Terwilliger.

When off the gridiron, one of Penland's fondest memories was spending time on a Nebraska farm. Penland and his brother often accompanied then-teammate Greg "Fletch" on trips to the Fletcher farm. "Matt and I were good friends with Fletch and we often went back home with him to his family farm in Oxford, Nebraska. Some of my best memories were of feeding the cattle, fixing fences, riding motorcycles and hunting."

By 1995, Penland was ready to close out his Husker career in style. "During senior day at the Oklahoma game I felt like it was time to celebrate. I had persevered for four-and-a-half years and was graduating in a few weeks. I was about to bring closure to one important aspect of my life and take on new challenges," expressed Penland. After completing yet another undefeated regular season, Penland and the Huskers were ready for the 1996 Fiesta Bowl.

"It was neat for a Florida native to have the chance to end his career against a Florida school. My family thought it was funny hearing all the Gator fans talk about how Florida would march up and down the field on Nebraska." In the weeks leading up to the Fiesta Bowl, Aaron's father Dave proudly displayed a

Nebraska flag on a highly visible bridge near the Gator Bowl in Jacksonville. Penland also had some extra incentive for wanting to share in defeating the Gators.

"Florida ignored me in the recruiting process so I was definitely hoping our team would play well," said Penland. The Nebraska versus Florida matchup also meant a high school reunion for Penland and Florida offensive lineman Elijah Brown. The two were teammates at University Christian High School, where they won two state championships. "It was neat how we played on the same high school team and then went on our own paths before being united at a national championship game."

The Huskers silenced all doubters with one of the most impressive college football performances, thrashing the Gators 62-24 to claim the school's second consecutive football national championship. "I definitely felt proud to be a Husker. It was great to see such tremendous fan support. To have three-fourths of the stadium at a neutral site filled with Nebraska fans was amazing."

Aaron Penland will never be accused of not giving his all during his Nebraska career. "Football has been a big part of my life since I was eight years old. It will be tough dealing with the end of competitive ball. I'm looking forward to working for my father's truck company." Penland earned his degree in Business Administration before playing his final football game.

Aaron Penland did not take the easy road through college. He did it the hard way and prevailed for the Cornhuskers. He gave up a scholarship at a Division IAA school to play for one of the best programs in the country. He will long be remembered as one of the Cornhuskers "special" players.

54

AARON GRAHAM

Husker All-American and Academic All-American center Aaron Graham has a history of beating the odds and silencing his doubters. "It all started back in eighth grade when one of my friends was told by a coach that he thought I would never be able to play at the high school level. Comments like that motivated me to work even harder and prove people wrong. It seemed like I've always been at the bottom of the barrel working my way up," remembered Graham. Growing up in Texas, Graham had lots of work to do to reach his goal of becoming an impact player in both high school and college. "In junior high I ran the 40-yard dash in seven seconds flat which is basically a brisk walk. High school football in Texas is a big deal and I knew I'd really have to hit the weights and work on my agility in order to have a chance of playing."

In fact, Graham went from being the fifth weakest player on his high school team at the end of his freshman year in high school to being the strongest by the end of his high school career. "I went from a bench press of 140 pounds to 380 in three years. I believe it was my determination and desire that allowed me to play as a high school sophomore," explained Graham. Despite starting for his high school team for two years and earning All-District and All-State honors, Graham was a virtual unknown to the so-called area experts. *"The Dallas Morning News* listed the top 500 metro football players and I was never mentioned throughout my entire senior year. I always make mental notes of disappointments like that and do my best to turn them into positives," said Graham.

Because he was snubbed by *The Dallas Morning News*, receiving a college football scholarship seemed highly unlikely for Graham. He, however, remained optimistic that he would play college ball and remembers receiving a letter from the Nebraska football program. "Nebraska was the first school to send me a letter and that opened the floodgates. I ended up receiving over 200 letters from virtually every Division I program," recalls Graham. "In the beginning, the recruitment process was exciting for me, my family and friends. Each day friends would ask if I got a letter from Lou Holtz, Tom Osborne or some other big-name coach or school. Then when the phone calls started, it became tiring and created lots of stress for a seventeen year old to deal with." Graham narrowed his list of colleges to three. He visited the campuses of Oklahoma, Texas Tech and Nebraska.

"The Nebraska official visit made all the difference in the world. You hear about the big weight room, the academic support, the facilities and the staff but it really makes an impression when you actually see everything in person. Coach Osborne was the other major factor in my decision. To have the man in my living room was a marvelous honor. My parents couldn't believe how quiet and reserved he was compared to most of the other coaches who were more of the 'rah-rah' variety."

The winter of 1990 found Graham on an emotional roller coaster. On the one hand, there was the excitement of recruitment and on the other, the diagnosis of his mother with leukemia. In choosing a school, he wanted to stay reasonably close to his family. In the end, it was Coach Osborne, the total Nebraska program and the proximity that made Nebraska the obvious choice for Graham. After signing with Nebraska and shortly before playing in the Texas Coaches' All-Star Game, which featured the state's 68 top players, *The Dallas Morning News* made a public apology to Graham for ignoring his obvious talent. "They did a feature story on me titled...WE APOLOGIZE TO GRAHAM! They admitted they had made a mistake when they totally overlooked me."

"I was so excited and relieved when I made the decision to go to Nebraska. I immediately began developing a strategy for reaching my goal of playing as a true freshman for Nebraska." Graham wanted both a head start on academics and athletics and made plans to enroll in summer school at Nebraska and begin the Husker strength and conditioning regimen. Shortly after solidifying his summer plans, Graham's mother passed away on May 3, 1991. "My father felt it was best for me not to deviate from the initial plan and I reluctantly went to Lincoln on June 5, 1991. It was a really tough time and the fact that I didn't know anyone in Lincoln certainly didn't help matters."

Graham's first year at Nebraska was eighth grade revisited. "In most ways I felt like I was at the bottom of the barrel again and needed to prove myself. I think the coaches felt I could become a good player but generally considered me a diamond in the rough." Graham was determined to beat the odds and become Nebraska's starting center as a freshman. Had it not been for a bout with mononucleosis, he was on track to reach that goal. After consulting with line coach Milt Tenopir, Graham opted to take a redshirt year in 1991 instead of using a year of eligibility as the primary back-up to would-be starter Jim Scott. "I felt I needed to get bigger and stronger and would go after the starting position my second year," recalled Graham.

Scott had a great 1991 season and retained his starting job for the 1992 campaign. "I couldn't beat the guy out. Jim matured into an outstanding center and earned All-Big Eight honors." Even though Graham and the coaches felt progress was steady, he wasn't satisfied playing back-up and began wondering if he would be one of those guys who might start only in his last season of eligibility. "I remember having a conference with the coaches and them asking me if I felt I could be an All-American. I told them 'Heck yes! I will be an All-American center' and that became a driving force for me." With the graduation of Jim Scott and two years of the NU system under his belt, Graham was convinced he could be the "center" of attention in 1993.

"The coaches moved Ken Mehlin from guard to center and to me that was hard to accept. I wondered if the coaches weren't certain I could handle the job at center as a redshirt sophomore." Although Graham played in all 11 games and was becoming regarded as one of the premiere deep-snappers in college football, it took an injury to lineman Brendan Stai to crack Graham into the starting lineup as center. Graham started the last four games of the 1993 schedule as well as the 1994 Orange Bowl game. After that he never relinquished his starting role throughout the rest of his Nebraska tenure.

Graham's first start as a rare sophomore center came in the unfriendly confines of Folsom Field against the Colorado Buffalos. Graham quickly erased any doubts that he could handle the role of starter, recording a season and team high 15 knock-down-blocks or "pancakes" against Colorado in a tight contest which was eventually sealed for Nebraska by a John Reece interception. The Huskers won the rest of the 1993 season games, earning the first of three consecutive berths in national championship games.

Graham was far from awe-struck about playing in the feature college game of the year. "I've been a dreamer my whole life and have always visualized going for the winning drive on a national championship team," said Graham. In addition to dreaming of national championships, Graham set goals to become an All-American both on the field and in the classroom. To his credit, he helped his Husker class win every Big Eight conference title and two national championships. Graham, his teammates and Coach Tom Osborne almost got their first on January 2, 1994. "It was a classic college football game filled with emotion and vivid memories," remarked Graham. The game also featured a fourth quarter debut of what was later dubbed as the offensive "pipeline." Brendan Stai made a miraculous comeback from a broken leg and closed out the game with Joel Wilks, Rob Zatechka, Zack Wiegert and Graham.

"Every day, during the last repetitions of practice, our line would say how this drive is for the national championship. I remember looking at the linemen in the huddle during the fourth quarter of the Orange Bowl and saying 'national champs.' Wiegert, Stai and Wilks just freaked and went nuts. Zatechka was staring into the crowd, probably thinking about chemistry. After getting Zatechka's attention, the line sprung redshirt freshman I-back Lawrence Phillips on a counter up the middle to draw NU closer to the national crown."

Just a few minutes later, deep-snapper Graham, holder David Seizys and place-kicker Byron Bennett had the chance to execute another national championship play. "We always practiced this every Thursday. Byron, Seizys and I would be the only three on the field at the end of practice. Since Byron and Seizys would run in from the sidelines, we would huddle and always say, 'this kick is for the national championship.' I'd snap it and we wouldn't leave until

Byron made the kick. He would almost always make it on the first attempt," recalled Graham.

With just over one minute remaining in a game for all the marbles, Seizys and Bennett took the field for the chance to give Nebraska a 16-15 edge over the Seminoles. "I told Byron, 'Hey we've practiced this a thousand times;' and I could tell by the look in Byron's eyes that he would make it and we would be national champions. After he made the kick it was chaos. Everyone had a difficult time remaining calm on the sidelines." Nebraska's celebration was short-lived. Aided by an out-of-bounds kickoff and late-hit penalty, the Seminoles and Scott Bentley regained the lead 18-16 with a successful field goal. The drama was far from over as the Frazier-led Huskers had one final shot at college football's ultimate prize. "After Trumane Bell caught a Frazier pass over the middle, I was immediately in the ref's face signaling for a time out. He looked at me and acknowledged the time out. Despite the pandemonium, I knew we had one last chance," explained Graham. After the official cleared the premature Florida State celebration from the field and put two ticks back on the game clock, it was *de ja vu* for Bennett, Seizys and Graham.

"When Byron came into the huddle, he was hyperventilating. After he kicked the field goal to put us ahead he ran up and down our sidelines living out his celebration ritual. Players were mobbing him on the sidelines. He also did the ensuing kickoff and, as a result, was out of breath and hyperventilating when he came into the huddle for the last effort for the title.

I looked at Byron and told him, 'You've got this —
national championship — no problem.' Byron was in
a daze and I don't think he heard a word I said. I had
an eerie feeling. I snapped the ball and the kick was
initially on line and then hooked like a golf ball."
Graham and the Huskers were heartbroken.

"I was totally devastated and wanted to rip the
turf out of the ground. I really felt like we should
have won the game," said Graham. Back in the sol-
emn Nebraska locker room, a dejected Graham
grabbed defensive lineman Christian Peter and said,
"We are coming back here next year and there is no
way we're going to lose like this again!" Graham's
words would prove to be prophetic as the Huskers
were motivated to take care of unfinished business.
Graham and his offensive linemen teammates wasted
no time on their goal to become the 1994 College
Football Champions. On January fourth, the line was
in the campus recreation center lifting and training;
their goal: becoming the nation's finest offensive line
in the history of college football.

If work ethic counts for anything, the 1994 Huskers were destined to become national champions. The
team had a burning desire with the total commitment
necessary to get the job done. With injuries to quarterbacks Tommie Frazier and Brook Berringer,
Graham and the 1994 offensive line became the "center" of attention. "We invited everyone to get on our
backs and ride the offensive line as much as necessary to win the title."

After coming so close the previous year, Graham

said the team felt pressure to make good on their goal of "finishing business" in 1994. "We didn't want to let ourselves down or Coach Osborne and the fans," explained Graham. The Huskers overcame seemingly insurmountable odds to claim their fourth consecutive Big Eight crown and set up a date with the Miami Hurricanes in the 1995 Orange Bowl. "There was never any doubt in our minds that we would win that game. We knew that eventually we would wear them down and take over the game," said Graham. Just as he had done one year ago, Graham had the chance to be part of a national championship drive. "There we were in the fourth quarter — game tied — and during a time out I told the line that this was definitely it. We would score and win the title." Like always, Wiegert and Wilks went bonkers; Zatechka was spaced out and something was wrong with Stai. I grabbed Stai's facemask and he looked up at me and said I had 'broken his damn foot.'" During the previous play Graham had inadvertently smashed Stai's foot by stepping on him with his cleated shoes. Stai hung tough and the pipeline paved the way for Cory Schlesinger to score his second fourth-quarter touchdown, ultimately giving the Huskers the 1994 College Football Championship.

"To finally win resulted in an unbelievable release in the locker room. We had come full circle. We had dedicated ourselves to one goal for 365 days and we did it. Everyone was celebrating — hugging and congratulating one another." Graham's emotion was captured on the cover of *Sports Illustrated* as he embraced tight end Matt Shaw after the 24-17 victory over the Hurricanes. "To be on the cover like that was just icing on the cake. I sent lots of copies back home and had one framed." With one national championship ring, Graham and the Huskers were now faced with the difficult task of defending the title and going for a repeat.

Graham's senior season as a Husker proved to be most memorable. Elected by his peers as one of five team captains, Graham became emotional prior to every game when he and his fellow captains walked out to the field. "It was unbelievable. Privately, I thought of my mother and wished she could have been there. I looked for my father in the stands and would point to him as the captains were taking the field."

Still, Graham enjoyed the '95 season. "The team knew what it was like to win and we wanted to do it again but we weren't going to stress ourselves over it like we did the previous year. No one thought we had a chance to repeat, so we really had nothing to lose," said Graham. The coaches were more relaxed and the players were in a better mood and that all made for a really fun year. Although, many found it difficult to categorize the 1995 season as a fun year. "The off-the-field problems were unfortunate, but in my eyes it was just as unfortunate to see how quickly some of the media and fans turned on us. We owe the doubters a thank you for giving us the extra incentive and desire to get back to the national championship game," explained Graham.

The 1995 Husker team adopted the team slogan, "Business as Usual." Aaron Graham's personal slogan has always been "Strictly Business." "Off the field I get along well with everyone and don't have any enemies. On the field I am all business and extremely competitive. If my teammates aren't working hard, or if they're bringing the team down by their words or actions, well then, I'm going get in their faces. Tommie Frazier and Christian Peter are two other players who had similar 'strictly business' on-the-field mentalities. If you got in the huddle and fooled around, Frazier would grab you by the facemask and tell you to 'pay attention.'"

After a string of off-the-field problems, Husker captains Graham, Christian Peter, Mark Gilman, Phil Ellis and Tony Veland feared the worst. "We thought Coach Osborne might do something drastic, like possibly quit. We all went to his office to visit with him — just to talk everything through. We wanted to lend our support and make sure he was OK." Osborne, Graham and the Huskers were more than OK as they dominated their 1995 opponents and won their fifth consecutive Big Eight Conference crown and the opportunity for back-to-back national titles.

"There was such a sense of confidence and unity on our team that I knew we would play well in the Fiesta Bowl." Upon arriving in Phoenix, Arizona, on December 23, 1995, for the '96 Fiesta Bowl against Florida, Graham felt the game would be close and probably determined by the better defense. As preparations continued and the coaches implemented the game plan, the Huskers became more and more confident. "In the Orange Bowl against Florida State we had some doubts about playing against Charlie Ward and the Seminoles. We thought we had a chance.... Last year against Miami, we believed we weren't going to lose the game, but there was still a 'what if' factor in the back of our minds. This year there wasn't a doubt that we would do well," concluded Graham.

Indeed, there was absolutely no doubt about the outcome of the Fiesta Bowl as the Huskers put the hurt on the Gators. "The first championship was definitely the sweetest and most emotional and the second time around I just tried to savor every last possible moment." Thrilled to be a part of back-to-back national championship teams, Graham was equally as proud of some of his individual accomplishments.

"I wanted to leave my mark as a total person on the Nebraska program. By becoming an All-American in the classroom as well as on the field, I hope I sent a message that I can keep things in perspective and follow through on my goals." Graham was also bestowed with the highest honor presented to a college student-athlete, earning Nebraska's twelfth NCAA Today's Top Eight award in recognition of academic excellence, athletic ability and citizenship.

Now the future appears to be bright for Aaron Graham. He's interested in careers related to animal science and ranching. When it comes to football, Graham feels he'll have to prove himself to the NFL. "I think there will be one team in the NFL who has faith in me and recognizes something special in me much like Nebraska did. Whoever that team is, I guarantee I will get the job done for them."

Aaron Graham has a history of rising to the top and beating the odds. He was a diamond in the rough for the Huskers and will continue his standard of excellence both on and off the field.

55

CHRISTIAN PETER

Like most people, Christian Peter has not been immune from experiencing "growing pains" in his life. Peter, who hails from Middletown, New Jersey, experienced a difficult transition process before getting a "wake-up" call that helped him mature into a co-captain for the 1995 Nebraska football team. The public has infinite headlines to choose from as they begin to reflect upon the departed Peter, however, before all final conclusions are drawn, one must come to know the person "Behind Every Champion."

Middletown, New Jersey, located thirty minutes south of New York City, is home to Hubert and Mary Peter and their children: Christian, Jason, Damian and Ashley. "My family is well respected and we are extremely close-knit. My mom and dad mean the world to me. They have constantly encouraged me and my brothers to get involved in sports," remembered Peter. He especially enjoyed swimming, soccer and ice hockey. He didn't start playing football until he was a junior in high school. One day at Middletown South High School, Coach Bob Generelli pulled Peter aside in the hallway. "Coach said I had good size and asked me if I wanted to come out for football. I said 'yes.' It was always something I wanted to do." Peter was a quick study in what turned out to be his only season of organized high school football. Peter earned All-State tackle honors on a team that went 9-0 on the way to a state championship. Peter was denied his senior season of football as the result of his transferring between schools as an underclassman.

After eighth grade, Peter had attended an all-boys school. "It was really a tough school academically, and it just wasn't working out for me. I decided to transfer to Middletown South. There things went well for me. The next year, my sophomore year, my father wanted me to give the all-boys school a shot again. I did and stayed there until November before being moved to a boarding school in New Hampshire. After I was there for a couple months I felt there was no way I could be successful. I was really happy to return back to Middletown South as a junior," remembered Peter.

Opposing high school coaches discovered Peter's transfers and notified the Board of Education, who ruled Peter would not be eligible to compete as a high school senior. "It was so confusing. I can't even explain it all. I think since we were number one and I played well, other programs were determined to find a way to keep me off the field," recalled Peter. Fortunately for Peter, he was able to participate in three scrimmages prior to his senior year. One scrimmage was taped and that footage became Peter's only hope of catching the attention of college football recruiters.

"In the beginning, it was never my goal to play college football. After I got a taste of football as a junior, it became something I got excited about," said Peter. Following an extremely successful junior campaign, schools nationwide began recruiting Peter until learning he was being denied his senior season. "Nebraska never backed off and I was flattered that they recruited me, considering they had so little to evaluate me on," remembered Peter. Eventually, Peter visited Nebraska and found everything was first class. "They had the biggest weight room, the best academic center and a great coaching staff. Put all that together, and it was really an easy choice to make." Peter gave some consideration to Temple primarily because of the proximity to his home.

Disappointed at having sat out his senior year of high school football, Peter was later sidelined again, this time as a result of academics. Peter failed to meet the NCAA Initial Eligibility Academic Standards and although he had enrolled full-time at Nebraska in 1991, he was unable to take the field. "It was really tough to be without football for back-to-back years. I began to question myself and wonder if I could make it in Lincoln and in the classroom," said Peter.

Peter faced some challenging obstacles. "I want people to know that I have a learning disability. I'm not a dumb kid. It's just that it can be very hard for me to concentrate for extended periods of time." Especially at the beginning of his college experience, Peter had a difficult time concentrating on much of anything. "I gained lots of weight in the beginning and got as high as 320 pounds. Things didn't get much better during my redshirt year in 1992; I had some behavior problems," remembered Peter.

Near the end of Peter's redshirt year, he received an ultimatum from Coach Tom Osborne. "Coach really gave me a wake-up call. He basically told me to change my act or leave. Nebraska was giving me every chance to be successful and I just wasn't responding," said Peter. "The talk with Coach Osborne was definitely the turning point in my career." After accepting support from Coach Osborne and others, Peter began to experience drastic improvements in all aspects of life.

"I started turning things around. I did better in school, lost weight and was beginning to feel good about myself," said Peter. Finally, after three consecutive years without the sport of football, Peter was ready for action as a redshirt sophomore in 1993. "It felt great to take the field again. I played quite a bit and made a contribution to the success of the team." In fact, Peter played in all eleven regular season games and the 1994 Orange Bowl. By the end of the season, Peter was backing-up nose tackle Terry Connealy.

Peter was quick to credit his turnaround to Coach Osborne and defensive coordinator Charlie McBride. "Coach Osborne got me pointed in the right direction and I guess you could say that Coach McBride was the man who fine-tuned me. In the beginning, I was flat-out terrified of the guy, but we came to enjoy a special relationship. Even though there were times when he would come down hard on me, he was just like one of the guys. McBride really loves his players."

Peter also came to enjoy special relationships with teammates. One who made an early favorable impression on him was fellow defensive tackle Kevin Ramaekers. "Starting in 1993, we roomed together and he was really good for me. Kevin had some ups and downs early on, but he made great strides. The coaches thought we would be a good match. Kevin was someone I really looked up to and learned a lot from. I have a great deal of respect for what he accomplished on the field and in the classroom." Peter named starting nose tackle Terry Connealy of Hyannis, Nebraska, as another positive influence. "Terry was probably one of the hardest workers I've ever been around. I tried to model his work ethic. Terry was one of the nicest guys off the field and one of the meanest on the field. I still can't believe we came from two very different worlds and became such close friends."

His relationships with Ramaekers and Connealy were helping him mold his college career, and he was determined to set the right example for his younger brother Jason, who was a true freshman in 1993. "I'm the main reason Jason came to Nebraska, and I was glad he got to see the new Christian Peter. I wanted to keep him from making the same mistakes that I did. I told him that as a Nebraska football player he couldn't consider himself just another guy. As a part of the team, he was going to be under the spotlight and maybe even held to higher standards." Peter expressed regret for how his Nebraska career started and was intent on not letting Jason fall victim to the same set of circumstances.

"I'll be the first to admit that when I came to Nebraska I was immature and made some poor decisions. I've never been a saint, but some of the major things I've been accused of during my career are not true. To me, it's sad that people can make accusations and ultimately tarnish a man for the rest of his life," Peter said. "Nobody really knew me or my background, but they made judgments about me based on the headlines. Ever since being labeled the 'Jersey bad-boy' I've been working hard to destroy that image."

As Peter earned more playing time on the field, the public and the Nebraska media began to see a different side of Christian Peter. "Once I was in the football spotlight people began to see my true personality and character. Opinions started to shift about me. I always tried to have a good relationship with the media."

In 1994 as a first-year starter at defensive tackle, Peter started every game on the road to the Huskers' first national championship since 1971. "It was great to play in the '95 Orange Bowl game and have my brother on the field with me," said Peter. Jason, also a defensive tackle, played special teams during the Orange Bowl. "We followed Coach Osborne's game plan to perfection. One thing I found out is you never question the big man. Coach is always right. It was just an unbelievable feeling when we won. I feel the unity and care our team showed for one another was the key to our perfect season."

Heading into his senior season, Peter was held in high esteem by many pre-season All-American teams.

Peter was also respected by his peers; he was elected as one of five 1995 team co-captains. "It was an unbelievable honor. I had turned things around to become a positive person and my teammates realized I made a 360 degree change. I feel most of my teammates could really identify with me. Everyone had room for improvement and I guess I offered hope to some of the guys. The players respected my work ethic and honesty." How would Peter respond to his new role with the defending national champions?

"I'd be lying if I said I wasn't nervous. There was pressure on me and the four other guys to lead the team. Our main job was to be there for the younger guys and keep the unity going strong." Peter was also called upon to motivate the Huskers prior to taking the field. "When it came time for the locker room talks, I was the man. I would let the four philosophers go first and then I would really get the rest of the players' juices flowing. I'd get in their faces and yell at them. I wasn't afraid to sacrifice my body for the team with whatever props I could find in the locker room. Light bulbs, chairs, head butts and screaming until I was red in the face."

In the beginning, Peter admits to trying to prepare his motivational remarks prior to the game. "The first couple of games I tried to plan a message in advance because I was so nervous. Toward the end, I used current issues and events to motivate the team. What a great thrill and honor to help lead the team," remarked Peter.

The 1995 season proved to be a challenging one to serve as a team captain. National scrutiny ran at an all-time high because of various off-the-field issues, some of which resurfaced from several years past.

"We were at the top of our game going into the 1995 season, and everyone wanted to bring us down. Coach Osborne and the players offered our story and most of the national media didn't care to hear our side. There were some very one-sided stories that came out," said Peter. The role of the captains was simple, according to Peter. "We supported everyone at all times. Some of us might have put ourselves in bad positions but the bottom line was none of us were bad people." One person that Peter was concerned about was his head coach, Dr. Tom Osborne. "I could sense the big man was down and I think he appreciated encouraging words from me. I'd tell Coach to hang in there and that we were all in this together. As a team we would come out on top no matter what people were saying about us or the program," explained Peter. If there was one person who enjoyed a unique relationship with Coach Osborne, Christian Peter was that player.

"When I first came to Nebraska, I had a hard time communicating with Coach Osborne. It seemed like we were on different pages. We have opposite personalities, but eventually we connected. I think over the years, just by being myself, he came to find me amusing." Peter considers Coach Osborne a man with a great sense of humor; at times the two would go back and forth at one another in good fun. "He has the best dry sense of humor I've ever been around. When I first met him, it seemed like he was a conservative gentleman. I take partial credit for bringing out his great personality and sense of humor. We've made each other laugh so hard that we were crying. At times, he could just look at me and make me laugh. I could always tell when he was about ready to bust out laughing because he'd turn as red as a tomato."

All jokes aside, Christian Peter and Tom Osborne developed a special relationship. "We developed a mutual understanding and respect for one another. I think we complemented one another well. I was very intense and emotional in the locker room. He saw some of my actions in the locker room and could sense I was really trying to get a theme or message across to the team. Coach Osborne knows who I am and what I'm about. The man respects me for my growth and I think he loves me unconditionally. I love him more than anything."

Peter also has great admiration for Coach Osborne for his coaching skills. "Coach uses a different approach. He has a way of building up confidence in the team. On rare occasions he gets emotional and when that happens he can really get my fire burning. A series of 'dadgummits' and I knew right then and there it was all over for the other team," remarked Peter. "Over the years I came to respect and understand his coaching style. He knows the game better than anyone and treats his players as humans. I believe he is the greatest college football coach in the history of the game," exclaimed Peter.

The Huskers and Coach Osborne finished the '95 season 11-0 and earned a spot in the 1996 Fiesta Bowl, the team's third consecutive national championship game. Peter and the blackshirts stifled the "fun and gun" Florida Gator offense and the Huskers rolled to a 62-24 win in the Arizona desert. "Winning back-to-back national championships, especially with all of the adversity we had been through, was very satisfying," said Peter. More importantly, Peter was hoping the nation would read between the lines. "Our team was truly a family in 1995. We supported and loved one another at all times. People were doing their best to break up our family, but we refused to let it happen. A caring coach with unified players can go a long way." Peter was especially proud to be a part of a senior class that many considered average at best. "Everyone talked about what a crummy recruiting class we had, yet most seniors walked away with five Big Eight titles and two national championships. I think we had only a few exceptional athletes in the bunch. We all worked extremely hard and believed in one another."

Team unity was vital. Peter also credits his family unity for his success. "I have the two greatest parents in the world. My entire family is the main reason I've made it this far." Peter has a special appreciation for his mother, Mary. "She is the backbone of the family and is such a strong person. It's been unbelievable what she has been through. It tears me up for my mother to have to hear some of the accusations people have made against me. My parents have never questioned my integrity and support me at all times," explained

Peter. Peter credits his father for instilling a tireless work ethic. "My father came over from Germany and brought a strong work ethic with him. His main message: 'If you work hard, you will get rewarded!'" The theory has worked for the elder Peter. He owns and operates the popular Fromagerie French restaurant in Rumson, New Jersey.

As Peter recollects, the family bond became even stronger during the summer of 1994. "Jason and I were attending summer school at Nebraska prior to the start of the '94 season. I remember being in my room at the apartment and Jason came in hysterical. He just kept saying 'Damian, Damian, Damian.' Finally, he calmed down and explained that our brother Damian was in a swimming pool accident and was paralyzed. My heart dropped and of course football was the last thing on our minds. We told the Nebraska coaches and jumped on the first plane back to New Jersey."

Damian Peter, a gifted 6-6, 310-pound sculpted athlete was at a friend's house in Jersey on a summer afternoon. While his friends were inside changing, Damian dove into the pool. "He banged his head where the shallow and the deep ends meet. He came back up for air, but then went straight to the bottom of the pool. His friends came out and at first thought Damian was joking before they dove in to his rescue. Paramedics helicoptered Damian to the nearest specialist."

Soon, Christian and Jason were at their younger brother's side. "To see our little brother who had been so successful in everything, lie paralyzed in a bed was a very helpless feeling. Nothing we could say or do would make him feel any better. That was without question the hardest thing I've ever had to deal with in my life," recalled Peter. The entire Peter family stayed by Damian's side. Seventy-two hours later, Damian started to wiggle his toes and fingers. "I knew then that he would beat this thing. He had strength and determination in his favor," said Peter. With each passing day, Damian made progress. "Doctors said it was a miracle and that he probably should have been in a wheelchair for the rest of his life."

After completing a grueling rehabilitation process, Damian recovered. He is now back in college and leading a good life. A sophomore on medical scholarship at Notre Dame, Damian is able to run, lift weights and is excelling in school. Damian will not play college or professional football like his older brothers. "Damian losing football was hard on the family. He was by far the best athlete in the family and had no limitations. Notre Dame had high expectations for him and felt like he would have been one of their greatest linemen ever," said Peter.

Damian's injury has put football in the proper perspective for his older brothers. "His injury makes Jason and I realize how fortunate we are to have football. I remember days at Nebraska when I was tired and didn't want to go all out. Then I'd think of Damian. Because of Damian, I never practiced lightly and always prayed for him before every game," Peter said. "Football can be taken away in an instant and should never be put in the same category as life."

Although optimistic about achieving his dream of playing in the National Football League, Peter has given thought to life without football. "I want to earn my college degree. Prior to Nebraska, many people said I wouldn't make it in school or would never graduate. I credit Athletic/Academic Director Dennis Leblanc for sticking with me through thick and thin. I remember there were times when Dennis and I would have some misunderstandings. He was always reporting to the coaches and my parents. There were times I became upset with him. In the end, he put me in a position to graduate and we became close friends," Peter said. "Dennis even named his second child after me. That tells you something about our relationship."

In the event pro football doesn't materialize, Peter hopes to follow in his father's footsteps. "I'd like to own and operate some type of restaurant back in Jersey with my two brothers. I think I have the work ethic and leadership to get the job done," said Peter. Or Peter may have yet another career option. "I could see myself becoming a dominant All-Star wrestler. I've grown up watching the sport and think I could put on a really impressive show."

After the victorious Nebraska Cornhuskers arrived at the Devaney Center in Lincoln following their second consecutive national championship win, co-captain Peter quoted champion All-Star wrestler Rick Flair. "'To be the best, you must beat the best!' It seemed like the most appropriate thing to say at a national championship tribute. If someone was going to be the new number one in college football, they would have to beat Nebraska and nobody has been able to do it for the last two years."

Many Husker fans will not soon forget a play involving Peter during Nebraska's Fiesta Bowl victory. The Gators had just scored a fourth-quarter touchdown and were attempting a two-point conversion when outside linebacker Jared Tomich came clean to knock the ball loose from quarterback Danny Wuerffel. The rest of the story can only be told by Peter himself. "I picked the ball up and started running like there was no tomorrow. By the time I got to the 50-yard line I was running on empty. Doug Colman was right behind me and I tried to give him the ball. He wouldn't take it so I decided to turn on the afterburners because everyone knows defensive tackles are the real skill position players. The strut and high step just happened and I could hear my teammates and the fans laughing as I was nearing the end zone. Even though the whole thing was called back, it is a memory I will never forget or live down."

People will be talking about Christian Peter for a long time to come. "I wish more people could get to know me as an individual outside of the uniform. There is definitely a side to Nebraska football players that the average fan doesn't know or hear about," said Peter. Few people know that Christian Peter is one of the first Huskers to volunteer for youth and community service programs. Peter has helped feed the homeless, visited hospital patients, youth groups, senior citizens, and "at-risk" adolescents. "I'm a caring person with many good qualities. My family, teammates and coaches know what I'm really about and that's what matters to me," said Peter.

Christian Peter will be the first to admit that he experienced "growing pains'" before and during his Nebraska career. The fact remains that Christian Peter overcame significant academic and athletic odds to mature into one of the most effective team captains in Husker football history. "I am very proud of the contributions I made to the Nebraska program. I owe so much to the loyal fans, the great coaches, counselors and my past and present teammates. I feel I am prepared for the roller coaster of life."

Luther Hardin Jr.

58

LUTHER HARDIN

In looking back on his lifetime, Luther Hardin can cite several "turning points" that have helped him achieve academic and athletic success. At the center of every turning point was Hardin's mother, Delores. "She is my role model because she has molded me into the man I am today," explained Hardin. Hardin also credits his father, Luther, Sr., for providing support throughout his life.

Hardin grew up in East St. Louis, Illinois, near the St. Louis metro area which is considered a tough inner city area and an area prone to tempting youth into wrongdoing. "I was definitely in with the wrong crowd during high school and fortunately my mother could see that," recalled Hardin. As a junior in high school, just when his football career was beginning to take off, Hardin was going to go out with two of his friends one evening. "My mother asked me not to go with them, so I stayed home," said Hardin. Late that evening, Hardin's friends were arrested and jailed for robbing a liquor store and shooting the clerk. "From that point on, I decided to try to do the right thing. Had I been with those guys, my life would have gone a different direction and I would never have had the chance to go to college."

However, college was definitely on the horizon for Hardin. He was introduced to football during his freshman year in high school. At that time, Hardin tipped the scales at 310 pounds and was one of only two freshmen who stayed with the sport his entire high school career. "All of the other freshmen were intimidated by the upperclassmen. I enjoyed being a part of something and felt that sports was a good way to stay out of trouble," reflected Hardin. Hardin, who played both offensive and defensive tackle, gradually emerged into a key player for Althoff Catholic High School. "I began to really dedicate myself to conditioning and started to play with intensity. By my senior year, I was down to 230 pounds and earned All-State honors," remembered Hardin.

Despite closing out his high school football career in stellar fashion, Hardin wasn't even thinking about college. That all changed when letters from various football powers began trickling in. "The college football recruiting process sneaked up on me. My first letter was from Indiana and I was very skeptical about their interest in me," said Hardin. Indiana and a host of other schools were impressed with Hardin's speed, power, frame and potential. In fact, Hardin was recruited by nearly every school in the Big Ten and Big Eight conferences before narrowing his final choices to Michigan, Indiana, Illinois, Kansas State and Nebraska. "After taking my official visits, my mother agreed that Nebraska offered the best total package. I really liked their academic support unit and felt like everyone I met was sincere and genuine," explained Hardin.

Nebraska head football coach Dr. Tom Osborne made an early impact on Hardin. "Coach Osborne really impressed me and my mother. He is a very honest man and everything he told me from recruitment to this day has been true." After committing to Nebraska, Hardin began preparing himself for the next major turning point in his life. "Once I made the decision to come to Nebraska, I really became scared about making the adjustment to college and to Lincoln. Simply put, it was a huge culture shock for me." Hardin credits the tight bond among the 1991 freshman class as one of the reasons he adjusted to Lincoln. "We really pulled together and all of those guys became my brothers." Later, Hardin joined Kappa Alpha Psi Fraternity and suddenly had several strong support systems in place. "Joining the fraternity was another positive turning point in my life. I began to network with others outside of the football team. I got to know career professionals and students nationwide." Just as the transition into Lincoln was challenging for Hardin, so was the initial jump from high school football to major college ball.

"The transition was heartbreaking for me and I felt like my pride was diminished. I went from All-American and Blue-Chip to holding blocking dummies. Every day the guys would tell me I was nothing but a rookie who would have to earn their respect on the field. I just tried to remember how everyone kept saying that things would get better after the freshman year and I was certainly hoping that would be the case."

During his freshman year, Hardin opted to redshirt and learn from the likes of Pat Engelbert, John Parrella and Kevin Ramaekers. "It was hard not playing that first year, but I knew it would take me a while to pick up everything," said Hardin. During 1992 as a redshirt freshman, Hardin was back in uniform and will never forget his first time running onto the turf of Memorial Stadium. "It was unbelievable. The older guys told me 'you are going to be running into a sea of red.' I was really nervous. I had butterflies all over the place," Hardin reflected. Every time Hardin took the field, he felt the crowd became his family. "My real family was only able to come to a few games each year. I wanted to always do my best for my family, my teammates and the fans," said Hardin. Hardin saw only limited action in 1992 and was certain 1993 would be a breakthrough year.

"But, 1993 was kind of discouraging for me. I felt like I was on the verge of being a blackshirt, but our talent was so deep I never really got the chance to show the coaches what I could do." Despite earning a letter, Hardin saw minimal duty but still managed to keep everything in perspective. "I never judged myself solely by what I did on the football field. Academic success was always very important to me and I knew that without academics there could be no athletics." In his third year at the University of Nebraska-Lincoln, Hardin was named to the "Grades & Glory" Academic All-American team and also received a student-athlete academic medallion in recognition of his commitment to the classroom.

"I worked hard at trying to be a positive influence on some of the younger players. I always made it a point to talk to the freshmen and stress the importance of academics. I told them that football would probably not be a part of their future plans but that a college degree would benefit them the rest of their lives!" Hardin and his 1993 teammates had the chance to make history in the 1994 Orange Bowl by claiming the school's first national crown since 1971.

"That game against Florida State was very devastating to me. It seemed like everyone that year was pulling for Bobby Bowden and Florida State and no matter what we did, they would still win the game," said Hardin. Hardin acknowledges that it was hard to stand on the sidelines and see his teammates put out their best effort, yet still come up short. "That game really motivated me to want to be a contributor and help put an end to all of the nonsense we read about in the papers. I couldn't wait to get back to Lincoln to start lifting and running again. Yes, everyone was disappointed but we were all motivated to get back to the national championship game," concluded Hardin.

As a junior for Nebraska, Hardin found himself playing outside linebacker. "The coaches felt my speed would be a better fit with the new 4-3 defense we were running. In some ways it was like starting all over from scratch. I had to learn new stances and plays. Luckily, I had some of the best to learn from like Trev Alberts, Donta Jones and Dwayne Harris. I took advice from each and tried to create a style that would help the team."

When starting quarterback Tommie Frazier suffered a blood clot in his leg, people everywhere began questioning if the 1994 Husker edition could indeed finish business and claim the national title. "I remember going to classes and having to reassure everyone that we would be OK and get the job done. Our team was so focused and determined as a result of the Florida State loss, that we had tunnel vision on a national title and wouldn't take 'no' for an answer under any circumstances." Hardin and the Huskers proved to be unified and focused with relatively unknown players accepting huge challenges and stepping up their performances. The Huskers outlasted all twelve regular season opponents as well as numerous much-publicized injuries and earned a return visit to the Orange Bowl. This time the opponents were the hometown Miami Hurricanes. Hardin was confident the outcome would be different from the previous year. "I just knew we were going to do it based on the practices leading up to the game. Coach Osborne and the staff had the perfect game plan and he told us that Miami couldn't handle the pounding we would give them, that we would eventually wear them down."

"As soon as Kareem Moss made that interception to seal the win, I was yelling and jumping for joy on the sidelines. It was so satisfying for the team and especially Coach Osborne! Coaches were yelling at all of us to get off the field," Hardin said. The Huskers were crowned the 1994 College Football Champions. Soon the focus shifted to 1995 and the hope for a repeat performance.

"I felt we had enough returning talent and that many of the guys were still hungry enough to go back-to-back. We had the 'refuse to lose' mentality and didn't want to give up the title," said Hardin. In the coming months, Hardin and the Huskers were not only defending the title but defending the program as a result of some highly publicized off-the-field incidents.

"It really disturbed me to see the way people were talking about our team and Coach Osborne. People were determined to tear down number one and I felt like everything was blown out of proportion," said Hardin. "Every player was assumed to be a criminal and guilty by association. Everywhere I went, I felt people were saying things behind my back and making judgments about me." Now a senior, Hardin was in a position to help quiet the critics through on-the-field domination. He was one of the top four outside line-backers playing backup to left outside linebacker and All-American Jared Tomich.

Hardin realized his full potential as a student-ath-lete in 1995, playing in every game. Against the nation-ally ranked Kansas State Wildcats, in front of his family, he snagged a deflected shovel pass and then ran three yards for a touchdown. "It seemed like the ball was in slow motion and fell right into my hands. It was great to do something special on homecoming in front of a national television audience and my family."

Hardin's last game was memorable. "Senior day was very emotional for me. I just never thought this time would come and then boom, suddenly I was playing my last home game. I wanted to remember every aspect of that entire day. I wanted that day to last forever." Prior to taking the field against arch-rival Oklahoma, the seniors made a brief stop to receive congratulations from Coach Osborne. "I thanked him and told him that I appreciated everything he had done for me and the team."

Another memorable moment for Hardin came on December 16, 1995. Hardin walked across the stage at the Bob Devaney Sports Center to collect his degree in Business Administration. "The diploma meant more to me than championships because I was living out the dream of my family. I promised my mother and grand-parents that I would graduate from college. I was so glad they were able to attend graduation and share in that very special moment," recalled Hardin.

Next up on Hardin's dream season was a trip to the Fiesta Bowl in search of a second consecutive national championship. "It was 'business as usual' and there was no way the team was going to be denied. The seniors wanted to go out on top of the college football world and we felt like a win was the only way to help Coach Osborne regain his credibility," re-marked Hardin. For the second consecutive year, the Huskers realized perfection. Nebraska throttled the Florida Gators 62-24 and sent shock waves through the nation as the team became the first to go back-to-back since Alabama accomplished the same feat in 1978-1979. Nebraska, however, is the first team to win con-sensus back-to-back championships in all major polls since Oklahoma did it in 1955-1956.

"I felt like I went out with a bang my senior year. I am leaving Nebraska with my college degree and seven championship rings. More importantly, I think I developed into a role model for others." Hardin, a regular volunteer through the Husker community outreach program, likes to talk to kids at "turning points" in their lives. "Kids are usually faced with choices — doing the right thing or doing the wrong thing. I tell kids to say 'no' to drugs, alcohol and gangs and to say 'yes' to education," said Hardin.

Luther Hardin is walking away from the University of Nebraska as a champion. Behind every champion is a person. Luther Hardin is a person who had the support of his mother and grandparents. Hardin made the most of key "turning points" and is now prepared to become a champion in life.

63

BRIAN NUNNS

Most athletes have a high degree of idealism concerning their athletic futures. Many are convinced that college athletics are a pit stop in preparation for a professional sports career. Husker journeyman offensive tackle Brian Nunns of Lincoln, Nebraska, has always been realistic about his career as a football player. "I've never been in a fantasy land thinking I would start for Nebraska or go on to play in the National Football League," said Nunns. Still, it was a dream come true to walk-on with the Nebraska football program. "Many of my coaches at Lincoln High had played for Nebraska and their advice was basically, if it's your goal to play for Nebraska, then go for it." Nunns credits the likes of ex-Nebraska football stars Mike Fultz and Micah Heibel for providing him with the encouragement and confidence to give Nebraska his best effort.

Nunns needed additional support after learning he did not meet the National Collegiate Athletic Association (NCAA) Initial Eligibility Academic requirements. That meant he was a victim of Proposition 48 and could not practice or compete during his first year of college. "It was horrible having to sit out that first year of college," recalled Nunns. "Once in a while I would walk by the field and sneak a peek at the team when they were practicing and that was difficult for me. My first year in college was spent going to class, attending study hall and lifting weights twice a day."

It was through weight lifting that Nunns was introduced to his eventual roommate and close friend Christian Peter, a defensive tackle from New Jersey. "Christian and I shared some things in common — he was also a Prop 48 and was very much into weightlifting," said Nunns. Nunns and Peter lived in the same residence hall during their freshman year of college and spent a lot of evenings together pumping iron. "We threw ourselves into the weights and the books, realizing how important both would be to our football careers."

After being sidelined in 1991, Nunns was more than ready to don the Husker red and white in 1992. "I was really coming in behind as a result of not practicing that first year and it showed. As a member of the scout team, I quickly earned the nickname 'helicopter.' The nickname was a result of an incident during practice with blackshirt and eventual pro player John Parrella. The coaches were telling me to be tenacious. I guess I slapped Parrella on his helmet and he didn't appreciate it." Apparently not. Parrella retaliated by grabbing Nunns' facemask and twirling him around like a helicopter. With determination and deep-rooted Husker pride, Nunns survived his first year of scout team and became convinced that all the effort was well worth it when taking the home field for the first time as a Husker. "It felt really good and kind of made my heart jump," recalled Nunns. "When they added the new sound system and the big screens we could hear the bass sounds in the locker room and that just made the team want to erupt."

Even though Nunns would have preferred to play a more active role on Husker game days, he remains convinced that regardless of playing time, just being a part of the Nebraska program and tradition would make him a better person. "The day of a football player is so full and demanding that by the time my day was over, I really had a feeling of satisfaction."

So the question often asked of Nunns and other Husker walk-ons is "why bother?" "Sure it is a ton of work but this program prepares you for life. You get far more than rings. You get lessons in life and make life-long friends." Throughout his Nebraska football career, Nunns developed many special friendships, most among his offensive line teammates. "The offensive line was a very tight group...like a bunch of brothers who would do anything for one another." One person that Nunns would do anything for is Christian Peter, from the defensive side of the football.

Nunns lived with both Christian and Jason Peter during his junior and senior seasons. "It has been great getting to know them and I only wish the public knew Christian and Jason like I do. Primarily due to a nationally televised news magazine program, most people expect Christian to be a thug and someone to stay away from or to fear," said Nunns. "Much to the contrary, Christian Peter is one of the most sensitive guys I have ever met. Of course around the stadium he presents himself as a macho, tough guy, but deep down he is a very caring individual. He is so good with little kids, especially his little sister. When he talks with her on the phone he is always telling her how much he misses her and loves her and says he will fly her out to Lincoln to go see movies like *Pocahontas* and *Operation Dumbo Drop*."

Nunns describes Christian and his brother Jason as clean freaks. "They both keep a spotless apartment and I'm sure that is something most people find really hard to believe." In fact, Christian often volunteers to do the cooking in exchange for Jason and Nunns taking care of all other household chores. Cooking runs in the Peter family, as Christian and Jason's father, Hubert Peter, owns and operates a French cuisine restaurant in New Jersey called Fromagerie.

The one quality that most impressed Nunns about Christian Peter was his intensity. "Christian was a great motivator for the team. He was always very intense and emotional in the locker room and able to get the team into a frenzy right before we took the field," said Nunns. "Christian kept us on edge. The players never really knew what to expect or what his actions would be. The bottom line was he gave us the confidence and fire to win."

Nunns highly respects Husker head football coach Dr. Tom Osborne. "He is a father figure to lots of guys on the team," said Nunns. "He is one of the most decent individuals in America and when the media began scrutinizing our program, they were critical of Coach Osborne and the team took offense to that," recalled Nunns. "Nothing had to be said, but you could just see the team pull together and become more determined to make a statement on the field."

The 1995 season was definitely a memorable one for Brian Nunns. After earning his first letter in 1994 and playing in three games as a junior, Nunns made the travel roster as a 295-pound senior and saw playing time in all but one of the Huskers' twelve games. "I would have never dreamed I would be a part of back-to-back national championships," said Nunns. "Considering the talent and work ethic of our team, no one should be shocked by what we accomplished. The repetition we go through in practice every day, the dedication in the weight room all year round was demonstration that we were trained to win at Nebraska."

The story of Brian Nunns and his Cornhusker career cannot be told without detailing his brief career as a member of the University of Nebraska wrestling team. In 1994, during his junior year, Nunns recalls eating lunch at the training table in West Stadium with the Peter brothers and some friends from the Husker wrestling team. Apparently, the Husker coaching staff was searching for a heavyweight replacement for All-American and eventual national champion Tolly Thompson during the upcoming Northern Iowa meet. "Coach Mark Cody was explaining why Tolly had to sit out and they were looking for a big guy to help out. Some of the guys on the team knew I had wrestled in high school and began encouraging me to do it. I guess I was a victim of peer pressure, and before I knew it, everyone convinced me that this would be no problem."

Little did Nunns know he would be going up against the second-ranked heavyweight in the country. Nunns remembered things getting off to a shaky start. "First of all, I'm a triple extra large and I was packed into an extra large singlet — I was smushed in there. But still, even after seeing my 6-7 opponent, I thought I would win the match." It was wishful thinking for Nunns as 56 seconds into the nationally televised match he was pinned. "The guy shook me like a Christmas bell and twirled me around for awhile and I don't remember anything else," said Nunns.

Nunns chose to block the memory of the event, but his football teammates were quick to remind him of the details. "When I got back to Lincoln, Christian and Jason had taped the match and couldn't wait to watch it with me and give me the 'business.'" In fact, one night the Peter brothers arranged to have the match shown at a popular downtown hangout during prime time hours. "It didn't bother me at all. It was all good-natured joking and, in a way, I guess you could say I took on celebrity status as a result of my wrestling career," explained Nunns.

Just when Nunns thought his stint as a wrestler was forgotten, he was the center of attention during the annual Husker Media Day workshop on the eve of the 1995 Nebraska Football Media Day. "The whole team was in the football auditorium and we were watching a video designed to educate us on how to deal with the media. Tommie Frazier was the guest host on the tape and he told the team, 'Whatever you do, don't embarrass yourself or your school on national television and then there it was again — my 56-second wrestling career. Everyone on the team busted out laughing. Coach Osborne laughed uncontrollably." Nunns was grateful about one thing. "Thankfully, they haven't shown the tape on the big screens in front of a packed stadium."

Brian Nunns has nothing but great recollections of his Nebraska experience. "I doubt if anyone will remember me down the road as much of a football player. What matters to me is that my teammates remember the effort I gave every day. I didn't just go through the motions. I worked hard and felt like I contributed to some of the best Nebraska teams in history."

Looking to the future, Nunns plans to teach and coach; he may explore the possibility of opening a fitness club. "It has always been a lifetime dream to own a club," said Nunns. Based on his past, people should know that Brian Nunns works hard to fulfill his dreams.

Steven J Volz

68

STEVE VOLIN

The name Steve Volin is synonymous with victory, dating back to an illustrious high school career in Wahoo, Nebraska. The school posted four consecutive undefeated basketball seasons and four straight state championships. Volin played a key role in those victories and he continued his winning ways when he walked on as a Husker in 1991.

"I always wanted to attend Nebraska and wouldn't even entertain other offers," recalled the 6-2, 290-pound offensive guard. Coach Osborne impressed me and my parents and I knew immediately that he was the type of coach I wanted to play for." Although excited about the opportunity to live out a childhood dream and play for the Cornhuskers, Volin had no delusions of grandeur upon arriving in Lincoln. "I knew I wasn't going to be the big man on campus and would have to really work on my speed and strength," said Volin.

Volin, who received GTE Academic All-American honors as a senior, had little problem adjusting to the college classroom compared to the challenges he endured on the field. "Two-a-days during my first fall camp were really trying and at times I wondered if it was all worth it. With the encouragement of my parents I decided to stick with it." As destiny would have it, Volin made the correct decision. He concluded his career with seven championship rings — five from the Big Eight Conference and two national championship rocks.

Persistence was just one of the life lessons Nebraska football taught Steve Volin. "I expanded my cultural diversity and came to realize that unity and teamwork would result in the achievement of goals." Volin also learned to give back to others, primarily through a big brother program initiated by Tom and Nancy Osborne called Teammates. "Basically, I just wanted to be there for my little brother as a friend and let him know that he could always count on me no matter what. It has been one of my most rewarding experiences in the last four years."

Volin was always behind his team, too. Nevertheless he was perplexed by the off-the-field incidents which generated negative publicity for the 1995 Husker team. "It was hard for me to understand how 147 guys could stay out of trouble and why three or four more couldn't. Then I realized that everyone has his own unique background and way of handling certain situations. It doesn't necessarily justify the problems but maybe can lead to an understanding of why these situations occurred and how to help prevent them in the future." Volin didn't consider himself a victim of the team's scrutiny, yet he expressed concern for Coach Tom Osborne. "The reputation of Coach Osborne and the program was threatened this past year and there was a moment when I thought the coach might walk away from it all." Shortly after the Lawrence Phillips incident, Volin vividly remembers a team meeting called by Osborne. "Coach Osborne's voice was real emotional and you could almost see tears in the man's eyes. It was a very moving meeting and seemed to pull the team back together."

The revamped 1995 offensive line was a key part of that pulling together. "The offensive line was highly motivated as Aaron Graham was the only returning starter from the 1994 National Champions and there were some doubters about our ability." The line silenced the critics en route to another rushing title as it amazingly didn't allow a single quarterback sack. "This year's line seemed relaxed and supportive of one another." Volin, who ended up playing in ten games during the '95 season and was on the travel roster, thoroughly enjoyed being a member of the offensive line. "I liked the mental aspect of the offensive line. It takes mental acuity along with strength and quickness to be a contributor." Volin was thrilled to be a part of the 1994 National Championship team but felt more a part of the team's win in 1995.

After claiming the big prize at the 1995 Orange Bowl, Volin said the challenge of a repeat provided ongoing motivation. "The team was motivated all year and the new offensive line wanted a title we could call our own," said Volin. Making the travel roster for the first time as a fifth-year senior also helped Volin feel more a part of the '95 crown. "Prior to this year it was

really a downer on away games. I'd practice all week
and then it seemed like I was temporarily discarded.
Everyone realized they were still a part of the team but
it was definitely a trying time." When Volin made the
travel roster, he felt truly comfortable in his role with
the Huskers. "Making the travel roster gave me greater
confidence and I knew I could get the job done when
called upon," said Volin.

The 1995 season culminated with an unforgettable
Fiesta Bowl performance against the Florida Gators.
For Volin, one of his best memories of the game was
being in on "the run." "Tommie Frazier always gave
everything he could on the field and his '96 Bowl
performance was a perfect example. On his spectacular
run, I initially blocked a linebacker; then after he
started to get piled up, the line just kept pushing
Tommie and tried to help keep him from falling. It was
amazing — he broke ten tackles on the way to the end
zone. Frazier is a great competitor. It was a lot of fun
playing on the 'O-line' with a quarterback like that. He
meant so much to this team because of his leadership
and confidence. We always knew we were in the game
with Tommie at the helm."

Like many of his teammates, Volin knows the impact of back-to-back national championships hasn't
been fully realized by the players. "When you are
involved with the program for five years, day after day,
you have high expectations. The achieving of those
goals is great but I think it will take a number of years
to finally understand the magnitude of what we accomplished." Volin and his teammates know the Husker

faithful are deserving of the right to savor consecutive national titles. "The fans mean more than they can ever imagine. They really helped charge up the team," said Volin.

Back in his home town of Wahoo, Nebraska, one would think Volin has taken on celebrity status as a result of his accomplishments as a Husker. "Not at all," said Volin. "Yes I am recognized, but I'm far from a hometown hero. People are nice and have congratulated me, but for the most part just let me go about my business."

Volin's business is no longer football as he prepares for his eventual career as a family physician. "I've accepted that football is over for me and I'm ready to move forward with my life. My ultimate goal is to be practicing somewhere here in Nebraska, possibly in Wahoo."

Steve Ott

69

STeve
OTT

Nearly all Nebraska kids dream of playing football for Tom Osborne and the Big Red. Henderson, Nebraska, native Steve Ott was no different. "I can remember playing football as a kid and imagining I was Turner Gill, Irving Fryar or Mike Rozier," recalled Ott. Like most Husker players, Ott was a standout athlete in high school, excelling in football and track and field. Even so, Ott was surprised when Husker Head Coach Tom Osborne came calling. "I really was concerned about my size since during my senior year in high school I weighed only 210 pounds." The Huskers were showing interest in him, but Ott was preparing to attend a smaller college. Like most in-state Husker recruits, Ott took unofficial visits to Lincoln during home Nebraska games.

In 1990, the third-ranked Huskers played host to the number two Colorado Buffalos. Ott saw one of the best games of the season; however, he never would have guessed that he would head back to Henderson with a scholarship offer. "I couldn't believe it — it was definitely the biggest day of my life!" said Ott. "Before one of the biggest games of the year at a pre-game function, Coach Osborne pulled me aside and told me I had the ability to become a great offensive lineman and a scholarship was available for me." There was absolutely no hesitation on Ott's part to accept the scholarship. "I have always had tremendous respect for Coach Osborne. He has one of the greatest coaching staffs in football." Ott was also impressed with the academic support provided to student athletes and the facilities, such as the multi-million dollar strength complex.

Weight training proved to be critical to Ott's transition from high school to big-time college football. "Immediately after accepting the scholarship to Nebraska I began pumping iron with the goal of weighing 250 or 260 by fall camp." Ott succeeded in getting bulked up to about 250 pounds but was still not prepared for what was in store during his first exposure to Husker football. As in most cases, Ott was put on the scout team matching him up against some of Nebraska's best defenders. "I was getting annihilated every play by blackshirts and current pro players like John Parrella who later played for the Buffalo Bills and San Diego Chargers. Scout team, according to Ott, is where one learns how to play Nebraska football. "You learn good technique and the ability to persevere."

Like many new freshmen, there were times when Ott was uncertain if he would last. "During the first week of two-a-days, I called home and told my Dad and my wife Michele I wanted to quit. I felt I was out of my league at Nebraska. My wife and parents encouraged me to stick with it, assuring me there would be more extreme challenges to confront in future years." Ott took the advice of his family and, like most, survived two-a-days and found that things only got better as time went on. In fact, one of Ott's most memorable moments came during practice as a scout team member when he got the best of black-shirt Kevin Ramaekers. "I was trying to make an impression on the coaches so I came off the ball quickly and drove Ramaekers on his back. I got up and was walking back to the huddle and he came up and smacked me on the side of my helmet knocking me on my back. He was ticked off and said, 'You are on the scout team and if you do that again, you'll regret it.' That was my true introduction to Big Red football."

During 1991, Ott opted for a redshirt season, realizing he still needed to mature physically and learn the mental side of Husker football. Ott, a standout scholar-athlete, quickly learned that Nebraska football was much more than X's and O's. Nebraska football, according to Ott, teaches about the game of life. Another lesson Nebraska football taught Ott was patience. "It was difficult going from being a high school superstar to basically being a practice player for three seasons," recalled Ott. "I learned how to take things day-to-day and focus more on team accomplishments than individual achievements."

Perhaps one of the most difficult lessons Ott learned dealt with adversity. After countless hours of dedication and practice, Ott meticulously worked his way up the depth chart, becoming the seventh man on the Huskers offensive line during his junior campaign in 1994. Ott was clearly becoming a vital cog in what was being regarded as one of the best offensive lines in college football. After playing in the Huskers' first seven games, Ott suffered a broken left foot during the Kansas State game all but ending his 1994 season. "That was definitely the lowest point of my career. Good things were starting to happen, and suddenly football was taken away. It was even more difficult having to watch the games from the sideline. The Colorado-Nebraska game was really hard to sit back and watch; all the players were so hyped up and all I could do was sit on the bench and watch the game from the big screens."

Rather than dwelling on the injury, Ott devised a strategy to make a traumatic experience into something positive. With a cast on his foot, he immediately took advantage of his extra time to further develop his upper body strength, looking forward to his senior year. Ott got the pins out of his ankle in early December; however, his injury prevented him from seeing action in the 1995 Orange Bowl game. "Not being able to contribute to that game was difficult and ultimately motivated me to work harder in the off-season to become a starter in 1995," said Ott.

In retrospect, Ott agreed that the foot injury was a blessing in disguise. "The injury helped me improve my overall strength and gave me a burning desire to win a national championship that I could call part of my own." Ott opened the 1995 season as Nebraska's starting right guard. He went on to start all eleven regular season games and was part of an offensive line that critics compared to the 1994 pipeline. Ott and the line paved the way for the Huskers to win their second consecutive and twelfth NCAA rushing title putting an end to critical comparisons. Ott also started in the 1996 Fiesta Bowl and helped the Huskers total a bowl record 524 rushing yards en route to the 62-24 victory. The Huskers' blackshirts recorded seven quarterback sacks against Florida in the Fiesta Bowl, but Ott and his teammates didn't allow a single quarterback sack the entire twelve-game season. Although Ott successfully overcame personal misfortune, he and his teammates were challenged early in the 1995 season by national scrutiny.

"It was really bothersome to me and my teammates that so many people began to question the integrity of the Nebraska program and Coach Osborne as a result of some highly publicized off-the-field incidents. Anytime a program gets to the top, people are always going to try to tear it down." Ott and the Huskers decided to use the continual negative publicity as a motivational tool to stay focused on playing perfect college football. "The team felt like it was our only chance to silence some of our critics and by playing great football, it would speak volumes about this team's character." The Huskers spent 1995 defending the title and the program. "I really felt bad for Coach Osborne because after the Lawrence Phillips matter, he appeared exhausted and drained." On the

Thursday before the Arizona State game, Ott remembered an emotional team meeting when Osborne nearly broke down. "Coach basically said, 'We simply can't have any more problems or our program might not ever recover.'" From that point on, Ott believes the Huskers were the most unified team in college football.

Steve Ott has had many championship moments during his Husker career. He is one of twenty-one Husker seniors who helped claim five consecutive Big Eight championships and back-to-back national championships. "My career has been filled with many bright moments." Ott recalls three occasions that evoke the most emotion in him. The first was taking the turf at Memorial Stadium in uniform for the season opener in 1992 against Utah. "It was an indescribable feeling and brought goose bumps to me. To walk through the tunnel and under the stands and have fans pat you on the pads and cheer for you is very moving. I believe it's the biggest adrenalin rush a person can experience. The sea of red and the roar of the crowd as you enter the stadium provided a memory I will never forget. Football Saturdays will be forever cherished. That was when all of the pain and sweat of spring ball, two-a-days and those grueling Tuesday practices paid off. For me, the games were also a time to see my family, including my brother from Seattle. He attended nearly every game of my senior season, in spite of the distance he had to travel."

The last time Ott took the field at Memorial Stadium was November 24th, 1995, against rival Oklahoma. "It was very emotional and I broke into tears because I realized this was the last time I would ever be in a position like that — a big chapter in my life was coming to an end." Added Ott, "Football has been the highlight of my life and even though that moment was very sad, it was very exciting and rewarding to have Coach Osborne acknowledge me for my five years of hard work."

The final time that Ott ran onto a field as a football player at any level was on January 2nd, 1996, in the Fiesta Bowl. "Coming out of the locker room and onto the field proved to the nation what our team already knew — Nebraska has the greatest and most loyal fans in college football. It was great to have a home field advantage and the crowd was definitely the twelfth man and they helped us defend the title."

Other memorable moments involved senior teammate and co-captain Christian Peter. Ott, like many players, credits Peter with providing some of the most emotional and vivid locker room talks in recent Cornhusker history. Ott remembers that during the 1994 season Peter was taking notes as then-captain Terry Connealy gave great locker room talks and Peter, on occasion, added remarks and motivation. Peter learned well from his peer and later made impressive talks himself. Traditionally, after all the coaches leave just before each game, the captains talk and try to fire up the team. "Prior to the Michigan State game, Peter smashed a light bulb on his shaved head and blood came pouring down his face onto his white jersey. Trainers had to come in and bandage Christian before he could take the field. I'm not certain what his intent was but it was a very moving talk that climaxed with the light bulb smashing," remembered Ott.

Steve Ott is well prepared to deal with life after football. Ott earned GTE Academic All-American and Academic All-Big Eight honors and graduated with a degree in biological sciences. Ott has accepted that his playing days are over and he knows he will miss being a Husker. "I understand football isn't forever and that's why I tried to make the most of my five years. I've learned lessons on patience, hard work, competition, teamwork and how to deal with adversity that will be with me forever. These lessons helped me be successful in football and will continue throughout my life. I have great memories and many close relationships to take away with me. Nebraska football will always be a part of me."

Steve Ott quietly matured into a solid Nebraska football player and Nebraska role model. "I believe all players must accept the role model challenge and recognize that someone out there, especially in Nebraska, is looking up to you." Although Ott had his share of sports role models, for him, his parents were his true heroes. "I especially idolized my father because of his work ethic, stability and values." Don't be surprised if youngsters identify Steve Ott as one of their role models. Steve Ott's Husker career has been an exciting roller-coaster ride. He started at the bottom as a 210-pound freshman scout team player and concluded his storybook career as a 275-pound starter for what became a team of champions. Steve Ott has many championship moments to remember from his days as a member of the Nebraska football program.

87

MARK GILMAN

As an adolescent, Mark Gilman frequently dreamed of becoming a professional athlete. Hoop dreams ran rampant for the Kalispell, Montana, native who, during high school, was regarded as one of the state's top basketball prospects and most talented all-around athletes. "Ever since my sophomore year in high school, I had dreamed of nothing but playing in the National Basketball Association," said Gilman. His father, Thomas, was a physical education teacher who allowed Mark easy access to the gym and an abundance of practice time. "Every free moment I had was spent in the gym," remembered Gilman. "I wasn't playing all the time to develop my game; it was just fun and something I really enjoyed."

Ironically, at about the time Gilman was maturing into one of the most-feared high school hoopsters, the Big Red football factory from Nebraska left a calling card. "During the summer of my sophomore year I got contacted by Nebraska at a camp and the coaches complimented me on my athletic ability. I was flattered but I told the coaches I was going to play college basketball. The staff said they would still follow me in the event my plans changed."

Gilman's interests took a different direction during his junior year. "Instead of shooting baskets in my free time, I began getting serious about weightlifting." Ultimately, it was Gilman's passion for weightlifting that helped him mature into an elite athlete.

During Gilman's senior year, schools nationwide started recognizing him for both his basketball and football promise. "I really wasn't expecting to get recruited in football. To me, it was just something to do for fun." Numerous schools made a play for Gilman, the basketball player, including Montana, Montana State, Army and Cal Irvine. And why not? Gilman was the most valuable player of the Montana State Tournament during his senior year and had a 20-points-per-game scoring average during his high school career.

He began to realize the Huskers were serious about him as a football player when Coach Osborne made a trip to Kalispell. "When he came, I was at a basketball camp in California. He really made a great impression on my parents." Although Gilman only took two official football visits, one to Nebraska and the other to Wyoming, he was recruited by all the PAC 10 schools. Nebraska clearly made the best impression on Gilman. Several factors made Nebraska the best choice. "I was astonished by the size of the weight room and thought everyone was very professional and business-like. The entire Nebraska program was awe-inspiring to an eighteen-year-old kid from the mountains of Montana. "Also, the sincerity and honesty of Osborne was something I really felt comfortable with." Gilman accepted Nebraska's scholarship offer and in the summer of 1991 made the journey from Kalispell, Montana, to Lincoln, Nebraska.

"The first thing I remember when getting off the plane in Lincoln was the humidity. It was like stepping into a giant sauna. Then I had to go through two-a-days that were almost unbearable," said Gilman. The humidity proved to be a minor adjustment compared to what he faced on the football field. As a high school player, Gilman played wide receiver during his sophomore and junior seasons and then quarterbacked for Flathead High School during his senior campaign. "The toughest thing for me in the beginning at Nebraska was getting used to blocking. The first time I got in a three-point stance was at Nebraska." Gilman estimated it took nearly two full years to learn the art of blocking — essential to the success of the Husker offense.

Gilman also struggled with accepting his role as a scout team player. "I went from being the go-to guy, the main man, to some dude at the north locker room who had a hard time getting a pair of socks," explained Gilman. He knew the transition to Big Red football would be tough, but nothing could have prepared him for going up against the likes of top defenders like Trev Alberts, Travis Hill, David White and John Parrella, all of whom graduated to the National Football League. "Some of those guys were very intimidating and only a few, like Trev, helped me up and provided encouragement," Gilman said. "The scout team really wasn't much fun. Getting knocked around all the time, I was wondering why I chose football over basketball."

During his redshirt freshman year at Nebraska, Gilman developed a special friendship with redshirt sophomore offensive lineman Brenden Stai. "Stai was another guy who was really dedicated in the weight room." In fact, both Gilman and Stai were so intense about their weightlifting, they would often go lift at the Campus Recreation Center after playing in Nebraska football games. "In looking back, it was the friendship and work ethic I developed with Stai that kept me from leaving Nebraska. Lifting with Stai also helped me get on the field. I mean, this guy was crazy about pumping iron. Stai was about 6-6 and 315 pounds. He bench pressed around 520 pounds and could squat a small truck," recalled Gilman. Stai also helped Gilman overcome his doubts about maturing into a contributor for the Cornhuskers. "There were times when I got pretty discouraged. I simply wasn't picking up the blocking. I gave serious thought to transferring and still trying to reach my basketball dreams."

Fortunately, Gilman opted to gut it out and went on to experience countless memories that would last a lifetime. The first of those memories came in 1992 as a redshirt freshman when he ran onto the turf at historic Memorial Stadium. "Stai tried to prepare me for what the 'rush' would be like. He said it would be like getting a permanent smile on my face and not being able to wipe it off." Stai's prediction came true for Gilman. "I just looked at the fans and smiled and hoped I wouldn't trip while running onto the field," remembered Gilman. "I'm sure few fans, if any, knew who I was but it was such a special day. I felt I was part of a big-time family atmosphere."

As a redshirt freshman, Gilman saw action in six games at tight end; however, it wasn't until his sophomore season that he recorded his first reception. "Back in high school, I would catch five balls a game and not think anything about it. With the emphasis on blocking, if I caught one pass a year at Nebraska, I felt like I'd won the lottery," said Gilman.

In 1994, as a junior, Gilman cracked the starting tight end rotation, splitting time with teammates Matt Shaw and Eric Alford. Gilman finished the regular season with 17 receptions and one touchdown. In the 1995 Orange Bowl game against Miami, Gilman snared a 19-yard touchdown pass from Brook Berringer which brought the Huskers within 3 points of the Canes. "When I caught that pass I almost had a heart attack in the end zone. What a feeling! The national championship game, 80,000 people in the crowd, millions more watching on televison and I was in the end zone with the ball in my hands. Time stood still for awhile," explained Gilman. "Of course the best thing was that we won the game and the title. I contributed and we won. I couldn't have written a better script."

Good things continued to happen for Gilman in 1995. In the spring, he won the Husker Lifter-of-the-Year Award for his work ethic in the weight room. "I consider that award one of my greatest accomplishments mainly because my teammates selected me; there were so many other deserving players." Gilman is quick to credit his weight room dedication as the primary reason he was able to make an impact at Nebraska.

In the fall of 1995, Gilman received perhaps the highest honor bestowed upon a Nebraska football player. He was elected as one of the five captains for the Husker team. "Being selected as a team captain made me feel good as a person. To me, it said my teammates thought I was fair, hard-working, supportive and goal-oriented."

Early into the 1995 season, Gilman and the other Husker captains were faced with additional team responsibilities, especially after running back Lawrence Phillips was suspended from the team. "We all worked hard to help keep the team focused on 'taking care of business' on the field. The scrutiny and negative publicity was very upsetting, but yet it seemed to have a positive impact on the team. Nothing really had to be said. We bonded closer together and tried to make a statement on the field."

Gilman was disappointed by the way Coach Tom Osborne was being portrayed in the national media. "Tom Osborne is one of the most spiritual, educated and genuine individuals I have ever known. Coach Osborne prepares his players for the game of life and I really respect him for that." Gilman has done his best to emulate Coach Osborne's character. "I believe once you sign on to be a Husker, you automatically become a role model." Gilman met the challenge at Nebraska, earning Academic All-Big Eight honors as a senior.

Just as Gilman accepted Osborne's role model challenge, his teammates responded to his pre-game locker room speeches. "Each captain had a very different approach. My message usually centered around unity, family, love and giving 110 percent on the field. I couldn't really prepare for the pre-game talks, it had to come from the heart. The locker room talks were very emotional."

A rush of feelings charged through Gilman as he took the field for the November 24th Oklahoma game, his last home contest as a Husker. "I tried hard to keep my emotions under control; there was still a game to be played," recalled Gilman. Nebraska's 37-0 shutout of Oklahoma capped the Huskers third consecutive undefeated regular season. "To me, that moment signified the end of a very good chapter in my life. Nebraska football helped me mature from a boy into a man."

After three days off, the Huskers resumed workouts in preparation for the 1996 Fiesta Bowl. "We had 23 practices before the national championship game. Our team felt prepared and I could sense a quiet confidence about the game. We expected to win and had a very 'business as usual' approach," remembered Gilman. Gilman and the rest of Coach Ron Brown's receiving corps took care of business with outstanding downfield blocking. "The receivers never got much hype. Coach Brown molded us into some of the best blocking receivers in the history of college football. Clester Johnson, Brendan Holbein, Reggie Baul, Tim Carpenter, Sheldon Jackson and the red-headed, mouth-smashing, human missile Jon Vedral, and I, created an all-out assault on the Florida defensive secondary," described Gilman.

After the Huskers dominated the Gators in every phase of the game to claim a 62-24 victory and second consecutive national title, the postgame reaction — compared to the previous title — was much different. "Nobody took the title for granted, it's just that all of the scrutiny was very draining and kind of tarnished a very special accomplishment," said Gilman.

The thing that Mark Gilman will remember most about his senior class and the Husker team was the sense of being among family. "I never saw much arrogance on any of the teams I played on. We just had dedicated people who represented the ideals of our head coach." As a result, Gilman fondly remembers the 1991 recruiting class earning five Big Eight championships and back-to-back national crowns. Fortunately for Mark Gilman and the Huskers, he bypassed his hoop dreams. Along with his senior teammates, he leaves Lincoln, Nebraska, with seven championship rings.

Jason Jenkins

96

JASON JENKINS

Jason Jenkins hails from Hammonton, New Jersey, which is thirty minutes from Philadelphia. A versatile athlete, Jenkins excelled in wrestling, football and baseball at Oakcrest High School in Mays Landing, New Jersey.

Jenkins credits athletics for helping him shy away from the constant temptations to get into trouble as a juvenile. "Some of the kids I grew up with are in trouble with the law or have drug problems. Some of them are successful like me. Most of those guys were great people who lacked the parental support that I had. They were often just looking for quick money."

Once Jenkins established himself as a top athlete in the area, the peer pressure to get involved with drugs and crime diminished. "Back in the neighborhood people won't mess with you if they know you have talent as a ballplayer. They respect your potential and don't tempt you quite as much."

Jenkins was, without question, a great ballplayer at Oakcrest High School. "It seemed like I did it all back then. I played fullback, defensive tackle, punter and kicker," remembered Jenkins. As a senior, Jenkins had the opportunity to play in the same backfield with his younger brother James. "As a freshman, he was the starting I-back and it was really fun opening up holes and blocking for him. People compared me to Christian Okoye from Nigeria because of my size, speed and strength." Jenkins earned All-Conference honors in high school and, not surprisingly, all of the big-time football powers were recruiting him.

"In the beginning, schools like Notre Dame, West Virginia, Miami, Oklahoma and Nebraska showed all kinds of interest in me," recalled Jenkins. Then came a setback that would alter the journey Jenkins would take after high school graduation. "I didn't meet the academic standards. I didn't have the test scores or the grade point average in the core courses. When schools found that out, almost all of them scattered." His high school football coach, Dennis DiDonato, encouraged Jenkins to consider attending a junior college.

"Coach DiDonato knew I had the potential to be a big-time player, so he helped me explore the best junior college football programs. I learned that the Jayhawk Conference was the strongest with schools like Dodge City, Coffeyville and Garden City. These were all schools that had pipelines to all of the major Division I programs." Jenkins ultimately decided to attend Dodge City Community College in Dodge City, Kansas.

"I liked the coaching staff and the facilities. For the most part I felt really comfortable there," said Jenkins. The transition from the East Coast to the Midwest was hard in the beginning. "Socially it was difficult. I had a hard time relating to people. It seemed like the tempo and language were quite different," remembered Jenkins. Yet, in the classroom and on the field, Jenkins made the grade. "I went from a 1.8 grade point average in high school to earning my Associate of Arts Degree with a 3.0 grade point average. I focused on school and football, knowing those two areas were keys to getting into a Division I program," explained Jenkins. He was a two-time selection to the first-team All-Jayhawk Conference team and was listed as one of the top 100 junior college recruits in the country in 1992.

"The recruiting process started all over again for me. I ultimately decided on Nebraska because they were one of the few schools who showed steady interest in me from day one. I really liked Coach Frank Solich and, of course, Tom Osborne," said Jenkins.

Jenkins arrived in Lincoln during the spring of 1992; he redshirted in 1993. "I thought I'd come to Nebraska and get on the field right away. But, I found out I needed to work on my technique and style." Jenkins added, "These huge guys and All-Americans were everywhere, so in looking back on the redshirt year, it was the best thing for me." That's not to say the redshirt year was an easy one for Jenkins. "At times it was very difficult and depressing. I thought about packing it in. I think the fact that I dealt with the adjustment to Dodge City, Kansas, helped me stick it out in Lincoln."

Finally, in 1994, the 6-5, 280-pound Jason Jenkins saw his first Division I action as a Husker. It couldn't have come in a better setting. "It was a really big deal for me playing my first game in the Kickoff Classic in New Jersey. I had a total of thirty family members and friends in attendance. It was neat that they could see me open my career with Nebraska. We played so well and shut out West Virginia. Winning was just icing on the cake," remarked Jenkins.

The 1994 Nebraska season continued the way it started. The Huskers battled opponents and injuries and finished 13-0 with a dramatic Orange Bowl win against Miami. "I was just thrilled to be a part of the number one team in college football. I was totally flabbergasted when we won and was really proud of everyone," said Jenkins. In fact, during the postgame celebration, Jenkins was hugging all of his teammates and carrying them on his shoulders. "I picked up kicker Tom Sieler and he was dangling up side down. I guess people thought it was neat because there was a picture of that in *Sports Illustrated* and *The Sporting News*," remarked Jenkins. This was just the start of some good times for Jenkins.

In May of 1995, Jenkins earned his college diploma from the College of Human Resources and Family Science. "Graduation was the highlight of my career. It was important for me to set an example for my younger brothers; I was the first in our family to get a college degree. I never thought I would get my college diploma." Jenkins was also thrilled that he earned his degree prior to the onset of his senior football season. "It took the pressure off and allowed me to concentrate more on football. I don't think the average person realizes how tiring it is to go to classes all morning, then meetings, practice and weights all afternoon. Then finally I would study until I couldn't stay awake any longer," explained Jenkins.

Heading into his final year of football in the fall of 1995, Jenkins was feeling satisfied with life. He had two of the best prizes a student athlete could dream of — a national championship ring on his finger and a college degree in hand. Unfortunately for Jenkins and the Huskers, the off-the-field problems of a few players resulted in scrutiny and investigation of the entire Nebraska program. The national media succeeded in finding a flaw in Jenkins' profile. Digging back to the spring of 1992, it was discovered that Jenkins was involved in an altercation and had charges filed against him.

Speaking of the incident in question, Jenkins recalled, "I was at a party when some guy started to cause trouble with me and then he took a swing at me. I ducked out of the way and in the same motion swung my left hand and connected. It was a natural instinct to defend myself and I didn't realize I had a bottle in my hand. The whole issue went through court and I paid the price for my actions. Then three years later it all became national news and I was portrayed as a big, mean, tough guy who walked around with his chest sticking out looking for trouble. Nothing could be further from the truth. I am a decent guy and a hard worker who has his priorities in order," said Jenkins.

"I realize after winning a national championship, that some of the media were determined to lump everything together from years back and present the most negative story." The aftermath of the negative publicity was difficult for Jenkins. "I didn't want to go anywhere because I knew most people were passing judgment on me. Nobody ever asked for my side of the story. I just dealt with the situation through isolation and thought in time things would quiet down," reflected Jenkins. "I am very sorry for what happened in the past and regret the whole experience," concluded Jenkins.

Throughout the difficult experience, there were several constants. "I always had the support of my family, Coach Osborne and my teammates," said Jenkins. "Coach Osborne supported me like a father. He was always there for me and is one of the greatest men I know." Jenkins also has great respect and love for his family. "I've always been big on family. I believe that supportive parents give you the chance to be successful in life. My parents have great morals and values and have always stuck with me through thick and thin." Jenkins' father, Paul Jenkins, a minister, has been very inspirational. "Whenever I really get down my father tells me to hang in there and he helps me realize that things aren't as bad as they may seem." Jenkins has always cherished the relationship he has with his father.

"Near the end of 1993, doctors found a blood clot in my dad's leg. They thought they might have to amputate his leg. He has diabetes and is on a dialysis machine twice a week. He gets very weak and each time I see him it looks like his condition is deteriorating. It upsets me. I want to be there for him all of the time just like he has been for me," explained Jenkins.

Jenkins was pleased to end his Nebraska career on such a high note by beating Florida in the 1996 Fiesta

Bowl. "Most people thought we couldn't do it. We basically silenced everyone and we were still standing tall in the very end. To me that tells me that our guys have unity and character," said Jenkins.

Jenkins is optimistic about playing professional football. "I know I will get the chance to show my skills and that is really all I can ask for." He is convinced his decision to come to Nebraska was one of his best choices ever. "I got the total package at Nebraska. The academic support is the best in the country and they have the caring counselors and graduation rates to prove that. I feel honored to have played for Coach Osborne and really appreciate his loyalty. Osborne gave me the chance to get a college degree and be successful in life."

☐ *Yes!* I want more copies of
BEHIND EVERY Champion...
($24.95 per copy plus $4.00 S & H
Nebraska residents add 6.5% sales tax.)

☐ *Yes!* I want a 15 X 22 Limited Edition
Full-Color Print
($15.95 per print plus $4.00 S & H
Nebraska residents add 6.5% sales tax.)

**Please send me _____ copies of the book
and _____ copies of the print.**

Send to: _____

Address: _____

City: _____ State: _____ Zip: _____

Daytime Phone: _____

Total: _____ ☐ Check Enclosed

☐ Or Charge My VISA/MasterCard (circle one)

Card # _____ exp. date _____

Signature: _____

Make checks payable to:

Dageforde Publishing

**941 'O' Street ▪ Suite 728
Lincoln, NE 68508-3625**

Or call Toll Free

1-800-216-8794